PEARSON

REALITY CENTRAL

Readings in the Real World

PEARSON

Upper Saddle River, New Jersey • Boston, Massachusetts
Chandler, Arizona • Glenview, Illinois • Shoreview, Minnesota

13-digit ISBN: 978-0-13-367435-4

10-digit ISBN: 0-13-367435-5

7 8 9 10   V011   12 11 10

TABLE OF CONTENTS

TABLE OF CONTENTS

 Unit 2 BQ: Is conflict always bad?

 Unit 3 BQ: What is important to know?

TABLE OF CONTENTS

 Unit 4 BQ: Do we need words to communicate well?

Unit 5 BQ: How do we decide who we are?

TABLE OF CONTENTS

 Unit 6 BQ: How much do our communities shape us?

ABOUT YOUR BOOK

The What and Why of this Book

This book is a collection of articles written with you in mind. The articles are on real-life topics you and your friends might talk about. In fact, you may even disagree about them. This is because the topics often have two or more sides.

The Big Question

The articles in this book are broken down into units. Each unit has a Big Question like this one: **How do we decide what is true?** After you read the articles in a unit, you will use them to answer the Unit Big Question. Each article also has its own main question for you to think about as you read. This question connects the article to the Unit BQ.

Unit Opener

Each unit begins with an opener that shows a real-life situation and connects to the Unit BQ. Use the opener to prepare for the unit articles.

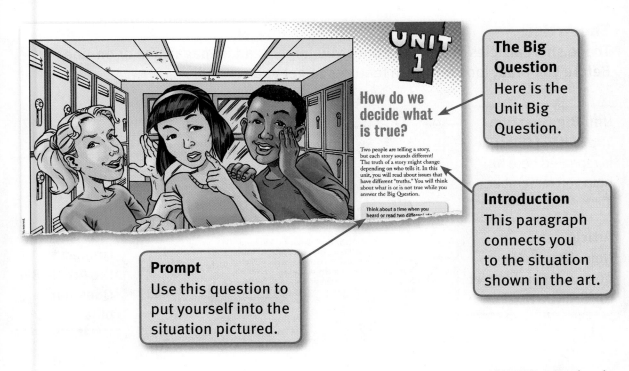

UNIT 1

How do we decide what is true?

Two people are telling a story, but each story sounds different! The truth of a story might change depending on who tells it. In this unit, you will read about issues that have different "truths." You will think about what is or is not true while you answer the Big Question.

Think about a time when you heard or read two different sto...

The Big Question
Here is the Unit Big Question.

Introduction
This paragraph connects you to the situation shown in the art.

Prompt
Use this question to put yourself into the situation pictured.

Kick It Off

Before each article you will find a Kick It Off page. This page will help you get ready to read the article.

Real-Life Connection
Use this section to think about the article topic. Here you may also see a graphic organizer to help you collect ideas.

Word Bank
Here are words that are important in the article. Notice that they are bold.

> **KICK IT OFF** A Place Where Strays Can Stay
>
> **Real-Life Connection**
> What do you know about animal shelters? You probably know that you can go to a shelter to adopt a pet. Ask yourself what animals go to a shelter and what happens to them once they are there. In a quick-write, jot down your thoughts on your own piece of paper.
>
> **Check It Out**
> What happens to shelter animals that are not adopted?
> - Open-admission shelters take all animals but "put to sleep," or gently kill, those that are not adopted after a certain time.
> - Limited-admission, or "no-kill," shelters take only some animals but do not put any to sleep unless they are dangerous or too sick to save.
>
> **decision** (di SI zhuhn) *noun* When you make a choice about something, you make a **decision**.

Check It Out
This section provides important information on the article topic if you need more background.

The Article

These short articles are like the ones you might read in magazines or on-line. Before you read, look for these features to get you started:

Unit Big Question
The Unit Big Question is repeated here to help you remember.

Article
Now the article begins. Do not forget to read the title!

> **THE BIG ?** How do we decide what is true?
> Half of all the animals brought to open-admission animal shelters are put to sleep. No-kill shelters seem like the answer to this sad problem. They may not always be the best choice, though. As you read the article, ask yourself: Are no-kill animal shelters really more humane than other animal shelters?
>
> # A Place Where Strays Can Stay
>
>
>
> Javier skidded to a halt and kicked his skateboard up into his hand. There was just one thing he had wanted for his birthday: a German shepherd dog. Yesterday, Javier went to the local animal shelter, hoping to find one. Instead, he saw a small, brown puppy with big, floppy ears. A woman had found the

Article Big Question
Use this section to connect to the Article Big Question in blue.

Read the Article

As you read the article you will notice several tools. These tools are here to help explain the article and to keep information organized and clear.

Subheads
Subheads help you preview what this section of the article will be about.

Vocabulary
Word banks terms and their forms are set bold to help you collect ideas.

Graph
Graphs like this one help to explain the ideas in the article. You may also see a chart or photograph here. Sometimes an important line or quote from the article will be featured.

THE FACTS ABOUT SHELTERS There are two kinds of animal shelters where unwanted cats and dogs are sent. One type is the open-admission shelter. Such shelters accept every animal brought to them. No matter how old, sick, or injured an animal is, they will care for it. Open-admission shelters always need more space. They can care for animals for only a set number of days. An animal that has not been adopted once those days have passed is euthanized. *Euthanize* means "to end the life of an individual as gently as possible for reasons of mercy." Shelters euthanize an animal by injecting it with chemicals that quickly cause its death. The other type of shelter is the limited-admission, or "no-kill," shelter. Such shelters do not usually euthanize animals. The animals stay at the shelters until they are adopted. However, these shelters can accept only a limited number of animals.

It may seem **unbelievable** that any shelter would kill animals. How can people who take in stray and unwanted animals also kill animals? The situation is not easy. Open-admission shelters work

HOMELESS DOGS AND CATS EUTHANIZED IN U.S.

Amount (millions)

1987 — 17
1998 — 5

Information is from American Pet Products Manufacturers Association, 2005–2006 National Pet Owners Survey.

Wrap It Up

After each article you will find a Wrap It Up box. This section is here to help you check your understanding and summarize what you have learned.

Find It on the Page
The answers to these questions can be found in the article.

Use Clues
You will have to use clues from the article and your own thinking to answer these questions.

> which shelters are the best option: open-admission or no-kill?

WRAP IT UP

Find It on the Page

1. Name the two types of animal shelters discussed in the article.

2. What are the main differences between open-admission and limited-admission shelters?

3. Summarize the main problem that all animal shelters face.

Use Clues

4. What do you think would happen if all shelters adopted a "no-kill" policy?

5. How would you solve the problems that no-kill shelters face?

6. What is your opinion of euthanasia as a solution to animal overpopulation?

Connect to the Big Question

After reading the article, do you think no-kill animal shelters are really more humane than other animal shelters?

Connect to the Big Question
Answering this question will help you connect what you have just read to the Article Big Question.

Unit Wrap Up

At the end of each unit you will find a fun project that will help you put everything you read together to answer the Unit Big Question.

Page 1

Project
This is the type of project you will be doing. All activities are done with a partner or in a small group.

Unit Articles
Use this list to pick articles that you especially enjoyed or want to think more about.

UNIT 1 WRAP UP

PROJECT: Interview

Answer the Big Question: How do we decide what is true?
You have read articles on issues open to debate. Now, use what you learned to answer the Unit 1 Big Question (BQ).

UNIT 1 ARTICLES

A Place Where Strays Can Stay,
pp. 4–7

Having Friends, Making Choices,
pp. 8–11

Smart Money,
pp. 12–15

Policing Changes,
pp. 16–19

Celebrity Scoop,
pp. 20–23

STEP 1: Partner Up and Choose
Your first step is to pick Unit 1 articles that you like.
Get together. Find a partner to work with.
Read the list of articles. Discuss which articles listed on the left side of this page were the most interesting to you.
Choose two articles. Pick articles that you both agree on.

STEP 2: Reread and Answer the Big Question
Answer the Unit BQ with your partner.
Reread the articles you chose. As you reread, think about the Unit BQ and how you decide what is true.
Interview your partner. Ask these questions about each article:
• What issue is this article about?
• What do the people in the article believe is

Unit Big Question
The Unit Big Question is listed here to remind you of what you will be answering through this project.

Page 2

Activity Steps
Steps are numbered with helpful directions and questions to walk you through the project.

...did you face? How did you decide what was true? Do you think you made a good decision? Explain why or why not.
Add to your notes. Add your partner's examples to the interview notes. Be sure specific details are included.

STEP 5: Check and Fix
Review the interview notes with your partner.
Use the rubric. Use the questions in the rubric on the right to evaluate your own work. Answer each question yes or no. Then trade interview notes with your partner and repeat.
Discuss your evaluations. Explain to your partner why you answered a question yes or no. For every no answer, explain what your partner could change to get a yes answer.
Improve your interview notes. If your interview notes can be improved, fix the mistakes or add more details.

STEP 6: Practice and Present
Get ready to present to your classmates.
Practice what you want to say. Use your interview notes to explain your partner's answer to the Unit BQ. Think about what you will say. Practice your presentation together.
Present your interview notes. Introduce your partner to the class and explain how he or she answered the Unit 1 BQ. Incl... least one specific example from an artic... and partner's own experien...

RUBRIC

Do the interview notes . . .
• have the titles of two articles from Unit 1?
• include an answer to the Unit BQ?
• give detailed examples from the articles to explain the answer to the Unit BQ?
• give at least one specific real-life example to explain the answer to the Unit BQ?

Rubric
Use the rubric to make sure you have included all the important information in your project.

Textbook Scavenger Hunt

To make the most of independent learning, you will need to use the unique features of this book on your own. Now that you have reviewed the features of this text, use this scavenger hunt to get to know your book from cover to cover.

With a partner or small group answer the questions below on your own paper. Use the walk-through on the previous pages as a quick reminder if you need it. Then share your responses with the class.

1 Turn to the Table of Contents. Scan to find an article that interests you. How can you find the article in the book? Turn to the article. What question will you answer as you read?

2 How are the topics in the index organized? Scan the index to find a topic that interests you. Then flip to an article that covers this topic. What do the captions, illustrations, and other visuals tell you about the article?

3 How many units are in the book? How can you tell? Flip through your book. Pause at the unit opener illustration you like best. How does it help you connect to the Unit Big Question?

4 Where will you find a Real-Life Connection with each article? Find one that includes a graphic organizer. What information will the graphic organizer help you to think about and organize?

5 What do the special quote features in this book look like? Find an article that features a quote. What information about the article does the quote give you?

6 Locate the glossary. Find a word that you do not know and share the definition with a friend. What other information about the word can you find in the glossary?

UNIT 1

How do we decide what is true?

Two people are telling a story, but each story sounds different! The truth of a story might change depending on who tells it. In this unit, you will read about issues that have different "truths." You will think about what is or is not true while you answer the Big Question.

> Think about a time when you heard or read two different stories about the same thing. How did you know which was true?

Real–Life Connection

What do you know about animal shelters? You probably know that you can go to a shelter to adopt a pet. Ask yourself what animals go to a shelter and what happens to them once they are there. In a quick-write, jot down your thoughts on your own piece of paper.

Check It Out

What happens to shelter animals that are not adopted?

- Open-admission shelters take all animals but "put to sleep," or gently kill, those that are not adopted after a certain time.
- Limited-admission, or "no-kill," shelters take only some animals but do not put any to sleep unless they are dangerous or too sick to save.

decision (di SI zhuhn) *noun*   When you make a choice about something, you make a **decision.**
EXAMPLE: *Adopting a pet should be a family **decision,** because everyone helps to care for a pet.*

fact (fakt) *noun*   A **fact** is something that is true.
EXAMPLE: *It is a **fact** that there are 5,280 feet in one mile.*

opinion (uh PIN yuhn) *noun*   An **opinion** is a belief based on facts and experience.
EXAMPLE: *Now that I have played both, it is my **opinion** that the first video game is better than the other one.*

unbelievable (uhn buh LEE vuh buhl) *adjective*   Something that is **unbelievable** seems unlikely to be true.
EXAMPLE: *This may sound **unbelievable,** but I have not missed a day of school since kindergarten!*

How do we decide what is true?

Half of all the animals brought to open-admission animal shelters are put to sleep. No-kill shelters seem like the answer to this sad problem. They may not always be the best choice, though. As you read the article, ask yourself: **Are no-kill animal shelters really more humane than other animal shelters?**

A Place Where Strays Can Stay

Javier skidded to a halt and kicked his skateboard up into his hand. There was just one thing he had wanted for his birthday: a German shepherd dog. Yesterday, Javier went to the local animal shelter, hoping to find one. Instead, he saw a small, brown puppy with big, floppy ears. A woman had found the puppy abandoned by the side of the road. It had been dirty, hungry, and alone. She had brought it to the shelter for care. "Who abandons an innocent puppy?" Javier wondered. This dog was not the German shepherd he had imagined, but it was a dog that needed a home. The **decision** was easy for Javier. He adopted the puppy from the shelter and brought it home.

Between 6 and 8 million dogs and cats are sent to U.S. animal shelters every year. Some of the animals are young and will be adopted at the shelter. Others may spend the rest of their lives there. Animals that are very old or sick are not likely to be adopted. What happens to them?

Animal shelters do their best to find loving homes for animals like this dog.

▼

THE FACTS ABOUT SHELTERS There are two kinds of animal shelters where unwanted cats and dogs are sent. One type is the open-admission shelter. Such shelters accept every animal brought to them. No matter how old, sick, or injured an animal is, they will care for it. Open-admission shelters always need more space. They can care for animals for only a set number of days. An animal that has not been adopted once those days have passed is euthanized. *Euthanize* means "to end the life of an individual as gently as possible for reasons of mercy." Shelters euthanize an animal by injecting it with chemicals that quickly cause its death. The other type of shelter is the limited-admission, or "no-kill," shelter. Such shelters do not usually euthanize animals. The animals stay at the shelters until they are adopted. However, these shelters can accept only a limited number of animals.

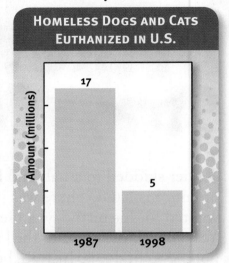

HOMELESS DOGS AND CATS EUTHANIZED IN U.S.

Information is from American Pet Products Manufacturers Association, 2005–2006 National Pet Owners Survey.

It may seem **unbelievable** that any shelter would kill animals. How can people who take in stray and unwanted animals also kill animals? The situation is not easy. Open-admission shelters work very hard to place animals in new homes. Unfortunately, too few people adopt animals from shelters. Shelters do not have enough room for all the homeless animals in the country.

IN NEED OF A HOME No-kill shelters might seem like the best place for unwanted animals. However, the **fact** is that these shelters face difficult situations, too. Many of these shelters do euthanize some animals. They euthanize animals that are very sick and cannot be cured. They also euthanize animals that pose a risk to people's safety.

No-kill shelters are usually full. These shelters must turn animals away. Homeless animals can face harsh, slow deaths. They may die of starvation or disease. They may be killed by cars or by other animals. Some people **believe** euthanasia is a more humane way for homeless animals to die. When animals are euthanized, they die with as little pain and distress as possible.

Animals in no-kill shelters may never get adopted. Unadopted animals spend their lives in cages. The Potter League, an open-admission shelter, presents the view that "keeping an animal caged . . . for months or years on end leads to animal suffering." In some people's **opinion**, euthanasia is a better option than such a life.

Sometimes, no-kill shelters are in a hurry to make room for more animals. One way they make room is by sending animals to foster homes. Doing this keeps the animals alive, but sometimes the foster homes are not checked out as well as they should be. An animal sent to a foster home may end up being abused or neglected.

It can be difficult to know the best place for unwanted animals. Sift through the facts to form your own opinion. Then **decide**. Which shelters are the best option—open-admission or no-kill?

WRAP IT UP

Find It on the Page

1. Name the two types of animal shelters discussed in the article.

2. What are the main differences between open-admission and limited-admission shelters?

3. Summarize the main problem that all animal shelters face.

Use Clues

4. What do you think would happen if all shelters adopted a "no-kill" policy?

5. How would you solve the problems that no-kill shelters face?

6. What is your opinion of euthanasia as a solution to animal overpopulation?

Connect to the Big Question

After reading the article, do you think no-kill animal shelters are really more humane than other animal shelters?

Real-Life Connection

You have been waiting all week to hang out at Melissa's house. Finally, your mom drops you off there, but the situation is not what you expected. Melissa's parents are not home. Older kids you do not know are there. If your mom finds out, you are in trouble. What do you do? Copy the chart below, and use it to jot down your thoughts.

Situation: You are at a friend's. Something is going on there that you don't like.
Response:

notice (NOH tuhs) *verb*   To **notice** something is to become aware of it.

> **EXAMPLE:** *It took awhile to **notice** the changes in Jim's behavior.*

prove (proov) *verb*   When you show that something is true, you **prove** it.

> **EXAMPLE:** *I emptied my backpack to **prove** that I had not taken the missing pen.*

study (STUH dee) *verb*   You **study** a subject when you read about it and think about it.

> **EXAMPLE:** *My brother never seems to have to **study** as much as I do, because learning just comes easier to him.*

test (test) *verb*   You **test** something when you try it to find out information.

> **EXAMPLE:** *If you really want to **test** your skateboarding skills, check out the new park.*

true (troo) *adjective*   Something that is real, and not false, is **true.**

> **EXAMPLE:** *It is **true** that our soccer team went undefeated this year, and you can check that out in the record book!*

THE BIG ?

How do we decide what is true?

Everybody wants to have friends. Naturally, you want your friends to like you. However, if you feel that your friends will like you only if you do what they want—that is peer pressure. As you read the article, ask yourself: What is the best way to handle peer pressure?

Having Friends, Making Choices

▲ Peer pressure can result in healthy choices, like studying with a friend.

Whom would you call your "peers"? *Peers* is a word that means "equals." They are people who are a lot like you. Not many kids hear their friends call them "peers." However, there is a good chance you have heard of peer pressure. That is when people who are like you try to talk you into doing the things that they are doing.

You probably did not realize this, but peer pressure can be a good thing! Think about it. Maybe you decide to go along for a team tryout when your buddies do. Maybe a friend encourages you to join a group to **study** for a big quiz. Seeing friends set and achieve goals can give you a boost.

However, in many cases, peer pressure can push you in the wrong direction or down the wrong path. Have you ever been in a situation in which you felt you had to **prove** yourself by doing something that you knew was wrong? Peer pressure can make a person afraid to speak up and possibly lose friends.

People may take dangerous risks because they do not want their peers to make fun of them. On the other hand, people facing peer pressure may be afraid to go along with a group. They may worry about getting in trouble with parents, adults at school, or even the police. By refusing to go along, however, they could be pushed out of the group.

▲ It can be hard to step away from the group and resist peer pressure.

What is the best thing to do if you find yourself in a tight spot? There are choices you can make when you feel peer pressure.

SAY YES Should you go along with the group? Of course, it is an option. Before you do anything, though, you need to think about the outcome. Stop and think *before* you say yes! It may help you to avoid making a big mistake. To **test** your feelings, try listening to your gut. In other words, **notice** how a choice makes your body feel. If the thought of saying yes makes you feel sick to your stomach, pay attention. Your body is offering **proof** that you are uncomfortable. A choice that makes you feel bad is probably not good! You are not being **true** to yourself when you go along with something you know is wrong.

SAY NO Saying no should be easy. The **truth** is that actually doing it in a difficult situation can be hard. Plan ahead so that you have a reason to back it up. "Oh, man, my dad said I had to be home right after school today. Sorry, I'm out." Say no, give your reason, and get moving! An exit plan, prepared ahead of time, is a good way to avoid a challenging situation.

STRIKE A DEAL You can stay with your friends and come up with another idea. Turn on the positive peer pressure, and rally your friends to do the right thing. Suggest that you go a movie or other safe place to have fun instead of somewhere that may lead to trouble. If no one wants to take your suggestion, that is okay. Remember your exit plan, and use it to make a graceful exit.

SLOW DOWN If you do not know what to do—do nothing. Tell your friends you will catch up with them later. When a situation comes up and you do not want to go along, say maybe or tell your friends you will think about it. You might want to say you are checking in at home first, and then stay inside and out of trouble. You can avoid an uncomfortable situation this way.

You may find yourself in a tight spot someday. Maybe you have already been there. There may be people around you making choices you know are wrong. Sometimes, it can be hard to know the right thing to do. You need support. Talk to an adult you trust about a situation you are facing. A coach, a teacher, an older sibling, or a parent may be able to help you decide the best way to handle it. You have got to put yourself first. Remember that **true** friends do not put you down when you stand up for yourself.

WRAP IT UP

Find It on the Page

1. How would you define *peer pressure*?

2. What is the difference between positive peer pressure and negative peer pressure?

3. Why is it difficult for some kids to say no to peer pressure?

Use Clues

4. What can you learn from facing a tough situation with peers?

5. How could you connect the ideas in this article to a situation in your own life?

6. Do you think it is possible to avoid being influenced by peer pressure? Explain your answer.

Connect to the Big Question

After reading the article, what do you think is the best way to handle peer pressure?

Real-Life Connection

One way to learn about money is by handling an allowance. A survey of parents found that about 60 percent of all U.S. kids get an allowance. Do you get an allowance? Are you expected to do jobs around the house to earn it? There are definitely advantages to getting an allowance. Can you think of any disadvantages? Copy the chart below to list your ideas.

Doing Chores to Earn Your Allowance	
Advantages	Disadvantages

WORD BANK

confirm (kuhn FUHRM) *verb*   To **confirm** something means to make sure it is true.
EXAMPLE: *The fact that Dwayne has good grades and a job should* **confirm** *that he is a hard worker.*

determine (di TUHR muhn) *verb*   When you reach a decision about something, you **determine** what to do.
EXAMPLE: *The doctor will* **determine** *whether I can play baseball again once I get this cast off my arm.*

intently (in TENT lee) *adverb*   To do something **intently** is to do it with strong focus.
EXAMPLE: *Wanda listened* **intently** *to the radio announcer, trying to hear the score of the basketball game.*

opinion (uh PIN yuhn) *noun*   An **opinion** is a belief based on facts and experience.
EXAMPLE: *My teacher says each person in class may have a different* **opinion** *of the novels we read.*

realistic (ree uh LIS tik) *adjective*   Something that is true to life is **realistic**.
EXAMPLE: *It is not* **realistic** *to expect to get all A's on your report card if you never study!*

How do we decide what is true?

"Aw, Mom. Do I have to take out the trash?" Reuben's mom sighed. "If you want an allowance, you've got to earn it." Reuben lifted the trash bag and grumbled, "My friend Andre gets $12 a week no matter what." As you read the article, ask yourself: **Do allowances help kids learn the value of money?**

Smart Money

All it takes is a trip to the mall to **confirm** the kinds of things people want. Stores display clothes, video games, and cell phones. How do you get the money for all this stuff? Unlike adults, you do not get paychecks. However, you might do odd jobs for cash or receive an allowance.

Some of your friends may earn an allowance by doing jobs around the house. They may earn even more money by working **intently** or by doing extra chores. They can spend money regularly, or they can save their dollars for a big purchase.

Other friends may get no allowance. Their parents pay for all necessities and give the kids "extras," or luxuries, as gifts. Alternatively, young people may do odd jobs for neighbors to earn some spending money. Either way, the kids probably cannot afford to spend money regularly.

Still others may receive a regular allowance no matter what they do. They do not have to earn it. Some people argue that this is not a **realistic** way to learn about money. There are many different ways to teach money skills. However, most parents have the same **intention:** to prepare their children to use money responsibly.

Some kids earn their allowance ▶
by doing household jobs.

FIRST PAYCHECK Doing household jobs is one way to earn an allowance. Chores might include washing dishes or walking the dog. Parents who use this system believe in connecting an allowance to chores. They hope doing this will prepare their kids to use money as working adults. A lot of people think earning an allowance is the best way to teach kids how to be accountable with money. This plan can have problems, however.

Earning an allowance might send the wrong message about work. It could lead to the idea that all jobs come with a price tag. Some allowance earners might refuse to help around the house unless they are paid. Others might not be interested in making money at all. They might decide not to do their chores. To them, folding the laundry is not **really** worth the money. Some parents think an allowance should not be a bribe or a paycheck. Everyone should do household jobs simply because he or she is a member of the family.

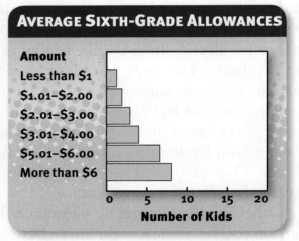

AVERAGE SIXTH-GRADE ALLOWANCES

Amount	
Less than $1	
$1.01–$2.00	
$2.01–$3.00	
$3.01–$4.00	
$5.01–$6.00	
More than $6	

Number of Kids

Information is from www.kidsmoney.org/allstats.htm.

MONEY FOR NOTHING In some families, parents give their kids an allowance no matter what. Every member of the family is responsible for doing certain jobs around the house. The jobs are not linked to the allowance, though. The parents believe that a regular allowance teaches their kids how to handle an income. They believe that the kids can learn how to budget money by getting the same amount regularly.

Other people disagree with this approach to allowances. They argue that it will not work when applied to life outside the family. Kids who do not earn their allowances might get false ideas. They might think they have a right to things they have not earned.

SAVING AND SPENDING Parents may find it hard to **determine** the best way to teach their kids money skills. They may wonder when to start giving an allowance and how much to give. They have to decide what they will teach their children about using and saving money. "Whenever a child says 'gimme,' you know he is ready to be taught to save," says Linda Barbanel, author of *Piggy Bank to Credit Card.* The amount of an allowance is up to parents. Many parents feel that $1 per year of life is the rule. Therefore, a child who is twelve years old would receive $12 a week.

Parents who give an allowance agree that it can teach good money sense. Many encourage their kids to deposit part of their allowance in a savings account. Some parents also teach their kids to set aside a certain amount of money for charity.

An allowance can teach important decision-making skills. It can help young people form an **opinion** about how to use their money. What about you? Do you have good money skills? If not, what can you do to improve them?

WRAP IT UP

Find It on the Page

1. Define the term *earned allowance.*

2. Summarize two different opinions about allowances.

3. What are the possible benefits of an allowance?

Use Clues

4. What might happen if kids skipped a job they were meant to do to earn an allowance?

5. What conclusions can you draw about earned and unearned allowances?

6. Pick one type of allowance and give your opinion of it.

Connect to the Big Question

After reading the article, do you think allowances help kids learn the value of money? Explain.

Real-Life Connection

Community policing is a type of crime prevention in which people team up with their local police officers for the good of the community. Some people believe building close relationships with police officers creates trust. Others worry that such relationships may lead to corruption. Corruption (kuh RUHP shuhn) happens when people change their behavior from making good choices to bad ones.

What do you think of community policing? Copy the chart below to complete the statement and explain your thoughts.

Statement: I think that community policing is a _____ idea.

Reasons:

WORD BANK

decision (di SI zhuhn) *noun*   When you make a choice about something, you make a **decision**.
EXAMPLE: *It is not hard for me to make a **decision** about which movie to rent, because I always get comedies.*

depend (di PEND) *verb*   When you **depend** on someone, you count on that person for support.
EXAMPLE: *Can I **depend** on you to bring the drinks to the party?*

evidence (E vuh duhns) *noun*   **Evidence** is any sign that something exists.
EXAMPLE: *The room showed no **evidence** of a robbery.*

examine (ig ZA muhn) *verb*   To **examine** something is to look closely at it to learn facts.
EXAMPLE: *The detective looked carefully around the room to **examine** it for clues.*

investigate (in VES tuh gayt) *verb*   To **investigate** something is to look at it carefully to find solutions or answers.
EXAMPLE: *I will **investigate** my options before choosing a topic.*

How do we decide what is true?

Think about the different tasks police officers handle. They do everything from writing parking tickets to working on SWAT teams. You may not think of them this way, but police officers also act as members of the community. As you read the article, ask yourself: **What is the true role of a police officer?**

Policing Changes

When you think of a police officer, what do you picture? You probably imagine a person who wears a dark uniform and a badge and carries a weapon. You may see officers patroling a certain area, or beat. You may see them driving through your neighborhood in a squad car. You may see them walking through the neighborhood. We know that police officers write parking and speeding tickets. They **investigate** crimes and collect **evidence** at crime scenes. The police protect a community in lots of ways. However, many people do not feel as if they *know* their local police officers. Should they feel this way?

What is the role of the police? Are they there just to enforce the law, or should they help citizens in other ways, too? How about helping an elderly person cross the street or walking someone home after dark?

These kinds of helpful activities are part of an approach to police work called community policing. Even though this approach may sound like a new idea, community policing is, in reality, very old.

▲
Police officers take on many different roles to keep a community safe.

One hundred years ago, before cars and motorcycles were common, many cops walked neighborhood beats. They would stop to check in on elderly neighbors. They would speak with local shop owners. In some cases, this closeness led to corruption. Slowly, as times changed, police officers became more removed from the people they worked to protect. Small local shops turned into big-box chain stores. Walking beats turned into patroling in cars. Some people felt this distance was good. It kept the police from getting too close to the community. Others disagreed. They felt the police had lost contact with the community they protected.

In community policing, local officers and citizens work together.

Now the role of the police in communities is changing again. Some communities are working to combine the old ways with the new. In community policing, local officers and citizens work together. They make **decisions** that help keep neighborhoods safe.

PARTNERING WITH POLICE You might think it means turning people in for arrest. However, there are many other ways community members and police officers work together. Some community members choose to attend a "citizens' police academy." There, they learn how to safely serve and protect their own communities. That knowledge prepares them to help officers **examine** and solve problems. The police **depend** greatly on citizens to let them know what is going on in a community. Police officers get involved in a community in lots of ways. One officer may coach a local sports team. Another may attend community meetings. Some people argue that such involvement distracts officers from their "real work." Others argue that it builds trust between the police and the community.

PREVENTING CORRUPTION Strong relationships between citizens and police officers can make communities safer. However, some people see potential problems with such closeness. They know that police officers who work closely with a community must work with all of its citizens—the lawbreakers as well as the law-abiders. They fear that such officers are more likely than others to become corrupt. Although corruption is not the norm, it can happen. Officers may take bribes. They may bend the rules for some **investigations** but not others. Police forces today watch officers and neighborhoods carefully to prevent corruption from happening.

THE PURPOSE OF COMMUNITY POLICING The goal of community policing is to keep people from committing crimes in the first place. "Prevention has always been a guiding principle of community policing," says former U.S. attorney general John Ashcroft. The hope is that officers who know a neighborhood will know how to help it. Officers and community members build trust and share ideas about how to solve community problems.

Community policing has expanded the role of police officers. Officers are not just observing from a distance. They are getting involved in a neighborhood's day-to-day activities. Although many people see the benefits of having police officers involved in their own communities, what potential problems can you see?

WRAP IT UP

Find It on the Page

1. What is community policing?

2. List two ways police can get involved in a community.

3. Summarize the types of problems that can come from community policing.

Use Clues

4. How has the role of the police officer changed over the years?

5. How might community involvement affect an officer's time and job?

6. How might corruption in community policing be prevented? Do you think it can?

Connect to the Big Question

After reading the article, what do you think is the true role of a police officer?

Real-Life Connection

Our rights protect our choices and set limits on behavior. What do you know about rights that have to do with privacy? Fill in a chart like the one below to find out.

Idea	Know a Lot	Know a Little	Know Nothing
The right to privacy			
The right to information			
Freedom of the press			

Check It Out

The word *paparazzi* (pah puh RAHT see) refers to a crowd of reporters or photographers who swarm like bees around a celebrity. Paparazzi comes from the name of a fictional character, Signor Paparazzo. In the 1960 movie *La Dolce Vita,* Signor Paparazzo is a street photographer. His name is from the Italian word *paparazzo,* meaning "buzzing insect."

WORD BANK

consequence (KAHN suh kwens) *noun*   A **consequence** is the outcome of a choice.
EXAMPLE: *The **consequence** for skipping practice is running laps.*

determine (di TUHR muhn) *verb*   When you reach a decision about something, you **determine** what to do.
EXAMPLE: *Our coach will **determine** if we play today's game.*

prove (proov) *verb*   When you show that something is true, you **prove** it.
EXAMPLE: *I can **prove** my age by showing you my birth certificate.*

true (troo) *adjective*   Something that is real, and not false, is **true**.
EXAMPLE: *You can check my facts to see that what I am saying is **true**.*

unbelievable (uhn buh LEE vuh buhl) *adjective*   Something that is **unbelievable** seems unlikely to be true.
EXAMPLE: *The rock star's rise to fame was **unbelievable**.*

How do we decide what is true?

Reading newspapers used to be the way most people got celebrity gossip. Today, anyone with an Internet connection, a cell phone, or a video camera can spread gossip. As you read the article, ask yourself: Do we have the right to know the truth about celebrities' lives?

Celebrity Scoop

Search for your favorite professional actor, singer, or athlete on the Internet, and you are sure to find a variety of stories. Some stories may be **true,** and some may be false. Do you ever stop to think about how celebrities end up in the news or whether the stories are actually **untrue?** Fame depends on public interest. However, does it mean giving up the right to privacy?

THE RIGHT TO PRIVACY Every U.S. citizen has the right to privacy. Basically, this right entitles people to be left alone. It means that the government cannot tell you what to do in the private matters of your life. It also means that you decide with whom you share the personal details of your life. Parents **determine** how to raise their children. Kids decide what to do with their free time. People choose whom they will or will not share their pictures with. However, what about people whose careers depend on the public's knowing who they are?

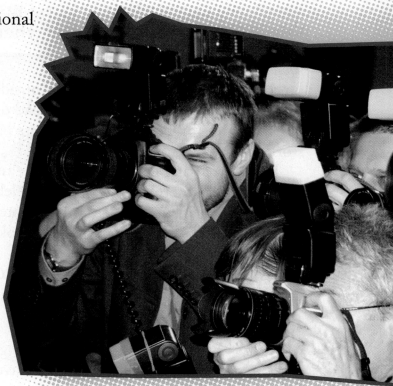

▲ **Some celebrities face crowds of photographers everywhere they go.**

Celebrities make a choice to be in the public eye. They need the attention of newspapers, magazines, and TV to advance their careers. The better known a star is, the more movie, concert, or sporting event tickets can be sold. Politicians get more votes if people know who they are and what they support. Celebrities willingly give up some privacy in order to be well known. They go to parties where their pictures will be taken. They pose for paparazzi outside movie premieres and other events.

However, they probably do not want to pose when they go out for a cup of coffee. You have probably seen pictures of celebrities on the beach, enjoying a vacation. Consider the negative publicity celebrities can get. Everybody has a bad day once in a while. The **consequence** for a celebrity of having a bad day could be seeing stories about it all over the news.

> **Must celebrities give up all their privacy, all the time?**

People tracking celebrities do some **unbelievable** things to get a scoop. Sometimes, they follow celebrities home and then post the celebrities' addresses on the Internet. "If you see George Clooney, you'll stare. But more than looking feels like taking. More than looking can feel like assault," says Michael Joseph Gross, author of *Starstruck: When a Fan Gets Close to Fame*. Must celebrities give up all their privacy, all the time?

THE RIGHT TO KNOW Many times, media companies justify their celebrity stories by saying they are giving the public what it wants. They argue that readers and viewers have a right to know what is happening in the world around them. Do we always, though? This argument may be right when it comes to news of key events. However, just how much about celebrities do we need to know?

The right to know personal information is really a myth. There is no right to information about celebrities' private lives. Yes, people may be interested in a famous basketball player. Fans do not, however, have a right to know what that player does off the court. Still, some people believe that the public does have a right to know the details of celebrities' private lives. These people point out that celebrities choose to be in the public eye. By making this choice, people argue, celebrities are inviting others into their lives. However, is all of a celebrity's life fair game?

FREEDOM OF THE PRESS The freedom of the press is a right that is legally protected. Public figures, like celebrities and politicians, expect to see themselves in the news. Many seek the attention. The fun stops for them when they see themselves in news that is **untrue.**

However, the press is protected, so celebrities have to **prove** it lied intentionally. Sometimes, they find getting **proof** or fighting the press to be too much trouble. Celebrities may let a false story go, unless they **believe** their reputation has been attacked.

A celebrity's right to privacy and the public's right to know collide when the topic is celebrity news. Although celebrities may seem larger than life, they are people, too. Does the public really need to know everything about their lives?

WRAP IT UP

Find It on the Page

1. Define the right to privacy.

2. Why would a celebrity want to give up his or her privacy?

3. List three examples of celebrity news that could be considered an invasion of privacy.

Use Clues

4. How does the public's interest level influence news content?

5. How much celebrity news do you read? Why?

6. How would you feel if photographers and reporters were constantly tracking you?

Connect to the Big Question

After reading the article, do you think we have the right to know the truth about celebrities' lives? Explain.

Real-Life Connection

What do you know about stage fright? How about its causes and symptoms? A symptom (SIM tuhm) is a physical change.

Copy the chart below. Then take a look at this list and decide which column each item belongs in: **pounding heart, fear of being onstage, fear of looking foolish, shaky voice, nervousness about doing something different, quickened breathing, worrying about being unprepared, stomachache.**

Causes	Symptoms
fear of being onstage	

audience (AW dee uhns) *noun*   An **audience** is a group that listens to or watches a performance.
EXAMPLE: *Most of the **audience** liked the play, but we did not.*

confirm (kuhn FUHRM) *verb*   To **confirm** something means to make sure it is true.
EXAMPLE: *Mr. Lou checked my homework to **confirm** my answers.*

fact (fakt) *noun*   A **fact** is something that is true.
EXAMPLE: *When I needed to find a **fact** about the Rock and Roll Hall of Fame, I went to the library.*

fantasy (FAN tuh see) *noun*   Something you imagine is a **fantasy**.
EXAMPLE: *My teacher always knows when I am dreaming up some **fantasy**, because she catches me staring out the window.*

fiction (FIK shuhn) *noun*   Something that is **fiction** is not true.
EXAMPLE: *I like to write **fiction**, because it is fun to make up characters.*

How do we decide what is true?

How do you feel when your teacher assigns a presentation? Annoyed? Frustrated? How about afraid? Many people dread the moment when they have to speak in front of others. As you read the article, ask yourself: **Are people's fears about public speaking grounded in truth?**

Fear in the Spotlight

Imagine standing just offstage in a large auditorium. Hundreds of people are in the **audience.** A microphone stands in the center of the stage. It is lit by a bright spotlight. The room is totally silent, because everyone is waiting for the speaker. The speaker is you. Everyone watches as you step up to the microphone to give a speech.

Does that situation scare you? Most people name public speaking as what they fear most. For some, this fear is even worse than the fear of death! This may seem like **fiction,** but it is true.

THE FACTS BEHIND THE FEAR You might think speakers with stage fright just fear being onstage. Stage fright is actually a lot more complicated, though. The **fact** is, for many people, public speaking is not a regular activity. Usually, your teacher is in front of the class. You and your classmates sit in your seats. A public speaking project is not something students do every day.

Some people find it frightening and stressful to be the center of attention. The focus is on one person standing in front of many others. When they look at the speaker, he or she may feel outnumbered.

▲ **For some students, giving a class presentation is no problem. For others, it is.**

Another thing that scares people about public speaking is the possibility of being made fun of. No one likes to look foolish. A presenter needs to be prepared for public speaking. Even a person who is fully prepared, however, can be afraid of failing. He or she may focus on all the negative things an audience might think.

Finally, the human body responds automatically to threat signals. A speaker knows that the audience is not out to hurt him or her. However, the

Notes and visual aids can help a speaker build confidence.

brain might see all those staring people as a threat. If so, it might activate the body's major threat response, known as "fight or flight."

FIGHT OR FLIGHT People once needed the fight or flight response for daily survival. A person facing an enemy or a charging animal needed to make a split-second decision. Such situations leave no time for problem solving, so the body responds automatically. Muscles contract, blood pressure goes up, and breathing speeds up. These changes give the body extra energy. They allow a person either to stay and fight or to run away fast.

Most humans do not regularly face the physical challenges they once did. However, the human body still has the instincts that helped it survive. "The fear of public speaking is more than anything a fear of being eaten," says speech trainer Mary Fensholt.

Even though we may understand that there is no **factual** threat, the body still reacts as if there were. A nervous speaker facing an audience may have trouble breathing. The voice can sound shaky as muscles tighten. The heart pounds as blood pressure rises. Other physical reactions can cause an upset stomach or dizziness. All these reactions add up to a case of stage fright.

IS IT REAL? Is stage fright real—or imagined? Many public speakers **confirm** that the feelings are real. The body's response to the fear is definitely real. The threat, however, is often nothing more than a **fantasy.** Most audience members are polite and excited to listen to a speaker. They are not on the attack. People who fear public speaking can remind themselves of this fact to stay calm. Speakers can also lessen stage fright by preparing thoroughly so that they know their material and audience.

Public speakers can try other strategies as well. They can make sure they feel familiar with the room they are speaking in. They might breathe deeply and slowly before beginning their speech. They can focus on relaxing their muscles. They can practice speaking in front of smaller audiences beforehand.

Many times, **confirmation** of a fear goes a long way toward taming it. Taking the time to step back and breathe deeply can really help. It *is* possible to deal with stage fright, if you know how.

WRAP IT UP

Find It on the Page

1. What is stage fright?

2. Summarize the reasons a public speaker might feel nervous.

3. How is the body's "fight or flight" response stimulated by public speaking?

Use Clues

4. What effects does the fight or flight response have on the body?

5. How could you use the information in the article to help prepare for a class presentation?

6. What is your opinion of the article's strategies to manage stage fright? Explain.

Connect to the Big Question

After reading the article, do you think people's fears about public speaking are grounded in truth? Explain.

Real-Life Connection

How do you get to know your friends? Copy the chart below and list in the appropriate column the things you do with your friends. As you read the article, consider these two ways of getting to know people.

Friends in Real Life	Friends Online

argue (AHR gyoo) *verb*   To **argue** with someone is to disagree with the person in a discussion.
EXAMPLE: *My mom will not **argue** with me about the rules because she says her word is final.*

constant (KAHN stuhnt) *adjective*   Something that happens over and over on a regular basis is **constant**.
EXAMPLE: *His watch was making a **constant** beep, and he did not know how to shut it off.*

fiction (FIK shuhn) *noun*   Something that is **fiction** is not true.
EXAMPLE: *Sam likes biographies, but my favorite thing to read is **fiction**.*

investigate (in VES tuh gayt) *verb*   To **investigate** something is to look at it carefully to find solutions or answers.
EXAMPLE: *We will **investigate** the plant's death by viewing its cells under the microscope.*

opinion (uh PIN yuhn) *noun*   An **opinion** is a belief based on facts and experience.
EXAMPLE: *I think the best time of day is morning, but not everyone agrees with that **opinion**.*

How do we decide what is true?

People usually become friends in person. They meet at school or in other face-to-face ways. People can, however, become friends without meeting in person. They meet on the Internet. Can you really know someone this way? As you read the article, ask yourself: **How do we really know someone?**

Facebook or Face-to-Face?

There is one thing twelve-year-old Kelly and her parents regularly **argue** about: MySpace. Kelly wants to set up her own page on the social networking site. Her parents will not let her.

Many young people use social networking sites like MySpace and Facebook. They use them to stay connected to their friends and to meet new people. Can you really get to know someone online, though?

A PEOPLE PLACE The Internet is a popular place for people to get together. Social networking sites give people a place to connect. Some people use the Internet to hang out with friends. Others use it to network for job opportunities. A writer might post a piece of **fiction,** hoping to get a company to publish it. A company owner could post job openings.

Whether people use the Internet for work or social reasons, networking sites serve one purpose.

▲ Spending time on the Internet is a common way for friends to connect.

That purpose is to allow people to share their interests. Social networking sites provide a place for people to share music and pictures, post messages, and update their profiles with facts about themselves. "Whether uploading a video, registering to vote, or catching up with friends, MySpace continues to be a central part of people's lives," says Chris DeWolfe, co-founder of the social networking site.

TYPES OF EMOTICONS		
Image	Keystroke	Label
😊	:)	smile
😉	;)	winking smile
😠	}: [	angry
😢	:' (	sad

How can you be sure about who you are hanging out with? Dangerous people can view profiles and collect personal information. It is a good idea to keep your profile private and to **investigate** the identities of other users. Once you know who you are chatting with, you can really start to expand your contacts. You can get to know people all over the world.

NEAR AND FAR The Internet has no geographic boundaries. In many people's **opinion,** social networking sites are a good way to get to know people in faraway places. You can learn about cultural differences and new ideas from friends online.

How well can you get to know a person you never meet face to face? You may or may not get to know the person well. Some people on social networking sites are dishonest in their profiles. They set up **fictional** identities. Some fake profiles are just for fun. However, other profiles are dangerous. You have to ask yourself, Do I really know this person?

Another drawback to these sites is the way people may communicate online. Most people send short messages back and forth. Communication is **constant.** It is also quick and informal. Think about your own use of these sites. Have you ever gotten into an **argument** on the Internet or tried to make a joke in a message?

A serious message might be misread as funny. A joke might not come across as you meant. You probably use emoticons like those in the chart to help you express your feelings. Still, without seeing a real face, it can be hard to know the emotion behind the words.

QUANTITY OR QUALITY Most profiles on social networking sites display the number of friends a person has. Building a long list of friends can get competitive. Are the people on your list really friends? How well can you actually get to know all these people?

Think about the things you do with your friends. You may play basketball after school. You may share an interest in reading or take an art class together. You spend time playing video games. You talk **constantly** on the telephone. All these things happen over time. It takes a while to get to know a person well.

Social networking sites can be a great way to keep in touch with the friends you already have. However, can solid friendships be built in cyberspace? In the end, it is up to each of us to decide.

WRAP IT UP

Find It on the Page

1. What are social networking sites?

2. Name two reasons young people use social networking sites.

3. What is a work-related reason that people use social networking sites?

Use Clues

4. How would you solve the problem of unknown users on a social networking site?

5. Do social networking sites improve the friendships you already have? Explain.

6. What is your opinion of social networking sites?

Connect to the Big Question

After reading the article, how well do you think we really know people we "meet" online?

Real-Life Connection

Spiders, needles, rocky cliffs. All these things scare people. For some people, they cause an intense and lasting fear. This kind of fear is called a phobia (FOH bee uh). Phobias are irrational fears. This means the fears are not based on facts or logic. What do you know about phobias? To find out, take a moment to write down all you know.

Check It Out

Who suffers from the irrational fears known as phobias? Look at these facts for some interesting information about phobias:

- Women are more likely to have phobias than men.
- Social phobias (fear of social situations) usually start when people are teenagers.
- About 8 percent of U.S. adults have a phobia.

evidence (E vuh duhns) *noun*   **Evidence** is any sign that something exists.
EXAMPLE: *My fever and red spots were **evidence** of chicken pox.*

quote (kwoht) *verb*   To **quote** someone is to repeat his or her exact words.
EXAMPLE: *We need to **quote** a primary source in our papers.*

realistic (ree uh LIS tik) *adjective*   Something that is true to life is **realistic**.
EXAMPLE: *The painting was so **realistic** it looked like a photo!*

study (STUH dee) *verb*   You **study** a subject when you read about it and think about it.
EXAMPLE: *At the library, I checked out books on World War II because I wanted to **study** the history of the war.*

test (test) *verb*   You **test** something when you try it to find out information.
EXAMPLE: *I want to **test** my cooking skills by making a new dish.*

How do we decide what is true?

If you forgot to do your math homework, you could blame arithmophobia (fear of numbers). Most people experience fear. Some people experience irrational fears known as phobias. As you read the article, ask yourself: Are phobias real or all in the head?

THE FEAR FACTOR

Imagine feeling fear so intense that it interrupts the activities of your daily life. You can't go anywhere far, because you fear riding in a car. Your fear of music prevents you from turning on the radio or listening to a CD. You have to ask everyone around you to be serious, because you suffer from geliophobia—fear of laughter.

Is there such a thing as fear of laughter? A fear like that might not make sense to you. Phobias do not make sense to many people. They are not **realistic** fears. Even so, phobias can keep people from leading normal lives.

Scientists who **study** phobias divide them into three main categories: social phobia, specific phobia, and agoraphobia.

SOCIAL PHOBIA Everyone feels shy once in a while. You may feel shy when you give a presentation in class. People might feel nervous if they think an audience is **studying** them. Sometimes, people get tongue-tied when they meet someone new. Social phobia goes way beyond these normal examples of shyness.

▲ **Arachnophobia is the intense fear of spiders.**

Social phobia is an extreme fear of feeling embarrassed or humiliated in front of other people. This fear can be so strong that it causes people who have it to completely avoid social situations. Such situations require people to interact with other people.

SPECIFIC PHOBIA A specific phobia is the fear of one thing. An extreme fear of flying, for example, is called aviophobia. Names exist for specific fears of cats and spiders. The most common specific phobia is a fear of a certain kind of animal. Lots of young children are afraid of dogs, snakes, or mice. Most kids, however, outgrow this type of phobia.

Someone with acrophobia could never ride this. Can you guess why?

AGORAPHOBIA Agoraphobia is the fear of being in a situation that might cause a panic attack. A panic attack involves sweating and difficulty breathing. People with agoraphobia have fears so strong that they avoid public places completely. Some agoraphobics never leave their houses. Others never even leave their rooms.

WHAT ARE YOU SO AFRAID OF? No matter what the phobia is, all phobias come down to the same thing: the fear of fear. It is normal to feel afraid sometimes. Experiencing fear can be OK. Fear can protect us from dangerous situations. Fear can help us **test** situations for danger. If we feel fear, we know to stop and think before we take action. Phobias, however, differ from regular fear. Phobias can get in the way of leading a normal life.

To **quote** psychologist R. Reid Wilson, "To be defined as a phobia, the fear must cause some level of impairment." This means that the fear must keep you from behaving the way you normally would. However, when you are feeling intense fear, it is very difficult to think straight. How, then, can you tell whether your fear makes sense or is simply irrational?

Evidence of a phobia includes feelings of panic and terror. People with phobias are unable to control the fear emotionally or physically. The body might react with a rapid heartbeat, shortness of breath, shaking, and a desire to get away from the situation. People with phobias will change their entire lives to avoid situations that bring on these **real** feelings of fear.

Phobias may not be based on logic, but they are real. The response they produce can be intense. Knowing this, you should always respect people's feelings, even if they seem silly or irrational.

WRAP IT UP

Find It on the Page

1. According to the article, what makes phobias irrational?

2. What is one difference between social phobia and agoraphobia?

3. How might one of the specific phobias mentioned in the article interrupt daily life?

Use Clues

4. What would you say to people who thought their fear was turning into a phobia?

5. Describe a situation in which fear can be helpful.

6. Evaluate the way the article gives information about phobias. Explain why you think the article is good or bad.

Connect to the Big Question

After reading the article, do you think phobias are real or all in the head? Explain.

PROJECT: Interview

Answer the Big Question: How do we decide what is true?
You have read articles on issues open to debate. Now, use what you learned to answer the Unit 1 Big Question (BQ).

STEP 1: Partner Up and Choose

Your first step is to pick Unit 1 articles that you like.

Get together. Find a partner to work with.

Read the list of articles. Discuss which articles listed on the left side of this page were the most interesting to you.

Choose two articles. Pick articles that you both agree on.

STEP 2: Reread and Answer the Big Question

Answer the Unit BQ with your partner.

Reread the articles you chose. As you reread, think about the Unit BQ and how you decide what is true.

Interview your partner. Ask these questions about each article:

- What issue is this article about?
- What do the people in the article believe is true? How do they decide what is true? Give a detailed example.
- What information in the article helps you to answer the Unit BQ: How do we decide what is true?

Take notes. Write the names of the two articles you chose. Take interview notes to record your partner's responses.

STEP 3: Discuss and Give Reasons

Talk with your partner about his or her answer.

Discuss your answer to the Unit BQ. Ask your partner to list reasons based on information he or she read in the articles:

- What details in the articles help you figure out how people decide what is true? What types of things do people think about when it comes to the truth?

Write your partner's answers. You can add these to your interview notes or use another sheet of paper if you want to.

STEP 4: Add Examples

Finish the interview by asking for real-life examples.

Prompt your partner. To get your partner to think even more deeply about the Unit BQ, ask your partner these questions about a real-life experience:

- How do you decide what is true? What problem or issue did you face? How did you decide what was true? Do you think you made a good decision? Explain why or why not.

Add to your notes. Add your partner's examples to the interview notes. Be sure specific details are included.

STEP 5: Check and Fix

Review the interview notes with your partner.

Use the rubric. Use the questions in the rubric on the right to evaluate your own work. Answer each question yes or no. Then trade interview notes with your partner and repeat.

Discuss your evaluations. Explain to your partner why you answered a question yes or no. For every no answer, explain what your partner could change to get a yes answer.

Improve your interview notes. If your interview notes can be improved, fix the mistakes or add more details.

STEP 6: Practice and Present

Get ready to present to your classmates.

Practice what you want to say. Use your interview notes to explain your partner's answer to the Unit BQ. Think about what you will say. Practice your presentation together.

Present your interview notes. Introduce your partner to the class and explain how he or she answered the Unit 1 BQ. Include at least one specific example from an article and one from your partner's own experiences. Consider using a multimedia tool to summarize your main points for your audience.

> ## RUBRIC
>
> **Do the interview notes . . .**
>
> - have the titles of two articles from Unit 1?
> - include an answer to the Unit BQ?
> - give detailed examples from the articles to explain the answer to the Unit BQ?
> - give at least one specific real-life example to explain the answer to the Unit BQ?

UNIT 2

Is conflict always bad?

When you hear *conflict*, do you think of fighting? Not every conflict is a fight. This conflict is about different ways of thinking or doing something. In this unit, you will read about conflicts between brothers and sisters and between friends. You will even read about conflicts people have with their own feelings. Think about the Big Question: Is conflict always bad?

> Think about a conflict you had with someone that you were able to solve. What did you learn from solving the problem?

Real-Life Connection

A family's birth order is the order in which children are born in the family, from oldest to youngest. Do you think people's place in their family birth order has anything to do with what the people are like? Does older siblings' behavior differ from younger siblings' partly because of being older? Read the statements below. Then copy them and write whether you agree or disagree with each statement. Explain your responses.

1. Birth order affects whether a person will be successful.
2. Birth order decides which child in a family will be the funniest.
3. Birth order has no effect on a person's life.

WORD BANK

argue (AHR gyoo) *verb*   To **argue** with someone is to disagree with the person in a discussion.
EXAMPLE: *Cliff and his sister always **argue** over which radio station to listen to in the car.*

compete (kuhm PEET) *verb*   When you **compete,** you try to win against someone else.
EXAMPLE: *Kenny plans to **compete** for the Most Valuable Player Award.*

instructions (in STRUHK shuhnz) *noun*   **Instructions** are directions telling you what to do.
EXAMPLE: *To build the model, Ned had to follow the **instructions.***

lose (looz) *verb*   When you **lose,** you fail to reach your goal.
EXAMPLE: *If we **lose** another game, our baseball team will be out of the championship series.*

negotiate (ni GOH shee ayt) *verb*   You **negotiate** when you talk with someone else to solve a problem through give and take.
EXAMPLE: *Maria and José will **negotiate** to decide who sets the table and who does the dishes.*

Is conflict always bad?

If you have a brother or sister, you know that siblings do not always get along. Is it possible that some conflicts happen because of people's place in their family birth order? As you read the article, ask yourself: **Does birth order always affect a person's life?**

Does Birth Order Matter?

Not many quarterbacks throw a football better than Peyton Manning. The 6-foot, 5-inch tall Manning led the Indianapolis Colts to a Super Bowl championship. Peyton's younger brother, Eli, also plays pro ball. He is a quarterback with the New York Giants. At first, fans said Eli could not **compete** with his brother's success. The Giants were known to **lose** too many games. That changed when Eli led the Giants to a Super Bowl victory.

Not many tennis players can hit a tennis ball harder than the Williams sisters. Venus is older and has won many tournaments. She is 6 feet, 2 inches tall. The ball jumps off her racket at more than 100 miles per hour. Serena is several years younger. She is also a few inches shorter than her sister. Serena is not as powerful, but she is considered one of the greatest tennis players ever to play the sport. She has won many more tournaments.

BIRTH ORDER BELIEFS Some people would say the achievements of the Manning brothers and the Williams sisters are due to birth order. These people believe that a family's first-born child tends to be a high achiever.

They believe middle children are usually rebels and that youngest children tend to be popular.

Venus (left) and Serena Williams celebrate winning a doubles match.

"Birth order is about coping," says Clifford Isaacson. He is coauthor of the book *The Birth Order Effect: How to Better Understand Yourself and Others*. Isaacson says there are no **instructions** for being a first, middle, or youngest child. We all must learn that our place in a family can determine part of our personality.

BIRTH ORDER AND PERSONALITY		
Firstborn or Only Children	**Middle Children**	**Youngest Children**
Are responsible and dependable	**Compete** to be noticed	Are creative and artistic
Are used to being the center of attention	Feel inferior to older siblings	Feel left out
Try to please parents	Rebel against the rules	Have a good sense of humor

Information is from *Time*, "The Power of Birth Order," Oct. 18, 2007.

Psychologists say many firstborns face pressure to succeed from their parents. They tend to be the parents' main focus until a brother or sister is born. These facts may help explain why firstborn children tend to be high achieving. Middle children have to deal with parents on the one hand and with siblings on the other. This position often helps middle children learn to **negotiate** conflicts. It can also help make them highly **competitive.** They tend to **argue** with older siblings and with parents. Youngest children can be the focus of the rest of the family. They can also feel lost while the focus is on older children. That may be why many youngest children draw attention to themselves with humor or artistic interests.

RECENT RESEARCH Researchers have found interesting facts about birth order. Firstborns tend to score higher on intelligence tests and are usually taller and healthier than siblings born after them. Firstborns also tend to be highly successful. More than half of all members of Congress are firstborns, as have been many U.S. presidents.

Studies show middle children can feel lost in a family. These kids tend to get less parental attention than firstborn or youngest children. They often are less self-confident than their siblings. They are also the most likely to get into **arguments** and become rebels.

In fact, one famous middle child was a leader of the American Revolution—George Washington.

Research has shown that youngest children are most likely to take physical risks. They are also most likely to get along well with other people. They tend to be the most emotionally sensitive siblings. This fact may help explain why many youngest children become artists or performers. Singer Mariah Carey is the youngest of three. Comedian Stephen Colbert is the youngest of eleven.

CAN BIRTH ORDER EXPLAIN EVERYTHING? Not everyone agrees that birth order is important. For example, one psychologist says, "I'm a middle-born, so that explains everything in my life—it's just not like that." Similarly, Serena Williams says she is motivated by sibling rivalry, not birth order. "No one gets me more motivated than [Venus], because I don't want her to catch up with me."

The Williams sisters are the youngest of five children. Eli Manning is the youngest of three. Peyton Manning is a middle child. Does birth order matter? What do you think?

WRAP IT UP

Find It on the Page

1. How are the Manning brothers similar?

2. List two qualities many people give to firstborns.

3. Summarize the problems that middle children might face.

Use Clues

4. Why might middle children be rebels?

5. Why might middle children tend to argue with older siblings and with parents?

6. If you could be anywhere in your family's birth order, where would you want to be? Why?

Connect to the Big Question

After reading the article, do you think birth order always affects a person's life? Why or why not?

Real-Life Connection

Think about the last time you had a conflict, or disagreement, with a friend. How did it turn out? Are you still friends, or did you drift apart? What do you know about solving problems you have with other people?

Copy the chart below. Then jot down your ideas for solutions to the problems listed.

Problem	Solution
Your best friend stops speaking to you.	
A boy you hardly know spreads rumors about you.	
A classmate wants you to skip class with her to avoid a test.	

WORD BANK

battle (BA tuhl) *noun*   A **battle** is a fight or struggle.
EXAMPLE: *The **battle** to decide who was the best rapper drew a huge crowd.*

defend (di FEND) *verb*   To **defend** is to protect someone or something from danger.
EXAMPLE: *Stephanie is determined to **defend** herself against Anton's gossip.*

explain (ik SPLAYN) *verb*   You **explain** something when you give its reason or background.
EXAMPLE: *Would you please **explain** to me why you were 30 minutes late to practice?*

negotiate (ni GOH shee ayt) *verb*   You **negotiate** when you talk with someone else to solve a problem through give and take.
EXAMPLE: *You want to go to the concert, but I want to go to the all-star game. Is there any way to **negotiate** so we can both be happy?*

resolve (ri ZAHLV) *verb*   To **resolve** something is to find an answer or solution to it.
EXAMPLE: *Padma decided to **resolve** her problem with her coach once and for all.*

Is conflict always bad?

Conflicts can range from arguments over who gets the remote on TV night to fights over a referee's call. There are many ways to handle conflicts, but it can be hard to know the best way. As you read the article, ask yourself: When should kids ask for help in handling conflicts with classmates?

DEALING WITH CONFLICTS

Has this ever happened to you? One day, somebody acts like your best friend. The next day, she points at you and says something to a big group. Everyone laughs. What is the problem? What can you do?

WHAT IS CONFLICT? Conflict happens when people want different things. Think about the situation above. Your friend may be mad because she thinks you have been ignoring her. She may be feeling insecure and trying to bring you down, too. She may be going through any of a dozen other problems.

A conflict with a friend can really ruin your day, but as strange as it sounds, conflict can be a good thing. It can lead to a talk about the problem. If both people are honest about what bothers them, it is usually possible to find a solution. Taking the time to **resolve** the conflict can help you to understand each other better. It can make the friendship stronger. On the other hand, it can show you that someone is not really your friend. If you can't work through the problem, it may be time to end the friendship. This possibility may sadden you, but it is good to know.

If someone will not look at you, he or she is probably upset with you.

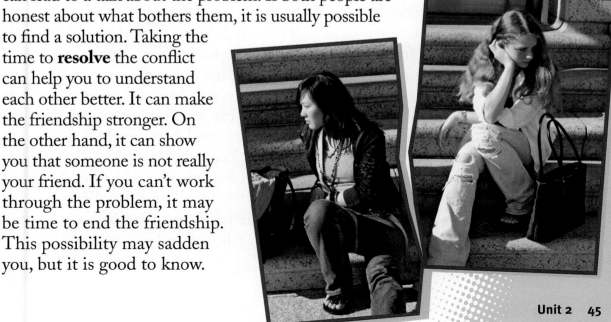

Conflicts can lead to change for the better. They may be uncomfortable, but they can teach us about ourselves. They can help you learn to **defend** yourself and ask for what you want. Conflicts can also help you to understand what other people feel.

DEALING WITH CONFLICT "No one is born with conflict-**resolution** skills," says psychologist D'Arcy Lyness. However, anyone can learn ways to **resolve** conflicts. Follow these steps.

Set the Tone. The first thing you should do is calm down. Take a few deep breaths. You might even walk away for a minute. Taking a break can help you figure out your own feelings.

> Conflicts can lead to change for the better.

Listen Up. Second, listen. Really hear what the other person is saying. Try to understand why he or she is so upset. After the other person finishes speaking, take a minute. Do not respond right away. Think about what you have heard and what you want to say. Then speak calmly. When it is your turn to talk, you have the same right to be heard respectfully.

Give and Take. Third, **negotiate.** Work together to figure out a solution. **Negotiating** means you have to give up something. The other person will, too. In the end, though, you should both feel comfortable. The decision should work for everyone.

Think about the three steps you just read. Suppose you are arguing with your friend Len. You are in science class showing your project, a model volcano. Yours works, but Len's does not. Len is clearly upset. He worked hard on his, too. He leans over and pushes your volcano onto the ground. He just ruined your science project on purpose. You are surprised and hurt, but before speaking you stop and take a deep breath. You calmly ask Len why he did that. You hope he will **explain** his behavior. If he does, listen carefully and try to understand. What if he does not? What if he just walks away? That is OK, too. He may need time to cool off and think. Do not try to force him to talk before he is ready.

What if Len does not answer your question and he gets angrier? What if Len's reaction scares you? You do not want a **battle,** and you are not sure what to do.

ASKING FOR HELP It can be difficult to know when to handle a conflict on your own and when to get help. Asking an adult for help can feel like telling on someone. The truth, however, is that some conflicts are just too big or too complicated. If the other person seems really disturbed, if there is a risk of physical danger, or if you are not sure how serious the problem is, talk to an adult.

Sometimes, you will need an adult to step in directly. Other times, you will need help solving the conflict yourself. The adult may have been through something similar and may be able to offer advice. He or she may be able to give an **explanation** that helps you understand the other person's side.

Dealing with conflicts can be tricky. It involves being honest about your feelings and really listening to someone else's. The next time you are in a conflict, remember that with time and patience, you can probably solve the problem.

WRAP IT UP

Find It on the Page

1. What is conflict?

2. According to the article, how can conflict be a good thing?

3. List three steps from the article that can lead to resolving conflicts.

Use Clues

4. Why is listening such a useful skill in resolving conflicts?

5. What would you say to a friend who asked you for help with a minor conflict?

6. Do you think the article gives good advice about how to resolve conflicts? Explain.

Connect to the Big Question

After reading the article, when do you think kids should ask for help in handling conflicts with classmates?

Real-Life Connection

What do you know about animals who save humans? Does this kind of rescue really happen? Is there actually such a thing as an animal hero? Take a minute to look over the statements below. Then copy them and write whether you agree or disagree with each.

1. Gorillas have saved children's lives.
2. Animals in the wild have raised human children.
3. Many legends tell about animals in the wild raising human children.
4. Animals in the wild can have feelings such as fear and stress.
5. Animals can think as well as humans can.

WORD BANK

challenge (CHA luhnj) *noun*   A **challenge** is a difficult situation to deal with.
EXAMPLE: *Len's energy sometimes makes sitting still a **challenge** for him.*

conclude (kuhn KLOOD) *verb*   You **conclude** something when you make a decision using the available information.
EXAMPLE: *If I see snow, I will **conclude** that it is time to get out my snowboard.*

direction (duh REK shuhn) *noun*   To go in a **direction** is to follow a certain path.
EXAMPLE: *We took a walk in the **direction** of the ice cream shop.*

lose (looz) *verb*   When you **lose,** you fail to reach your goal.
EXAMPLE: *Yasmin worked hard to get students to vote for her, because she did not want to **lose** the election.*

survival (suhr VY vuhl) *noun*   **Survival** means to stay alive in difficult situations.
EXAMPLE: *The **survival** of endangered animals depends largely on the choices of humans.*

Is conflict always bad?

When firefighters sacrifice their own safety to rescue people in danger, we say they are brave. What happens, though, when an animal saves a human life? Does the word *sacrifice* or *brave* apply to animals? As you read the article, ask yourself: What makes some animals help humans in times of conflict?

Animal Heroes

On a summer day at Brookfield Zoo, near Chicago, a three-year-old boy leaned over the railing at the gorilla exhibit. He leaned too far. Before anyone could grab him, the boy fell 18 feet into the exhibit. He hit the hard ground and did not move. Suddenly, a gorilla named Binti Jua ran in the **direction** of the little boy. People watched in horror. Would the massive gorilla crush the boy? Would the boy **lose** his life? No, Binti Jua gently picked up the little boy. She carried him to a door where zookeepers stood. The boy lived.

This story would not surprise some people. They believe that certain animals can think and feel almost the same as humans can. They point out the many stories in which animals have saved people in danger. What makes animals act this way in times of danger and conflict? Do animals have courage? Do animals have a special sense about danger? We bond with our pets, but what do we know about wild animals or animals in captivity? Can we **conclude** that animals and people are more alike than different?

▲
Binti Jua and her baby

STORIES PASSED DOWN For hundreds of years, people in different cultures have shared similar beliefs about animals and humans. Many stories tell about animals raising human children. In the early 1800s in France, newspapers reported the discovery of a "wild child" who had been raised by wolves. In the 1920s in India, newspapers published photos of "wolf children." Two sisters, Kamala and Amala, were said to have been raised by wolves.

Today, few people believe that animals could raise a human. The **challenge** to a child's **survival** would be too great, they argue. However, many animal lovers have seen pets show caring and loyalty toward children. Some people believe that animals in the wild can feel love, sadness, and anger.

For some animals, rescuing people is their job.

RESEARCH ON WILD ANIMALS Scientists have studied wild animals to look for proof that animals have feelings similar to those of humans. One possible proof is seen in elephant behavior. Elephants have been known to feed dying relatives in an effort to save them. Also, when relatives die, elephants may bury them and gather around the grave.

Some scientists believe that wild animals can think, too. One of the most intelligent animals is the crow. In one experiment, a crow picked up a straight piece of wire and bent it into a hook. It used the hook to lift food from a tube that was too deep for its beak. The bird had never seen a piece of wire before but used it to make a tool.

Psychologist Marc Hauser has studied animals all his life. He strongly believes that animals think. "Of course they do," he says. "How could they not think and . . . **survive** in the world?"

Hauser believes the main difference between animals and humans is speech. "Animals have thoughts," says Hauser, but they cannot speak. He says that when humans developed the ability to speak, they also developed higher levels of thinking.

Do animals sincerely care about humans? This is a **challenging** question. Some researchers have **concluded** that animals act only on instinct. These researchers think that animals are programmed to respond to danger and act. Other researchers argue that if animals were actually programmed to act this way, all gorillas would save humans and all dogs would alert people to dangers. Why do some animals act this way while others do not? Animal researchers are still trying to answer this question.

WHAT CAN ANIMALS "TELL" US? Most researchers are not surprised that animals have saved human lives. Researchers know an animal can be smart enough to sense danger. An animal can therefore act to save a person's life. By watching to understand why animals do certain things, we may be able to understand whether animals are acting on instinct or by choice.

Animals cannot speak. They cannot tell us why they do things. For now, we will have to draw our own **conclusions.**

WRAP IT UP

Find It on the Page

1. What did people expect Binti Jua to do with the boy who fell?

2. What did Binti Jua actually do?

3. What stories exist about animals raising children?

Use Clues

4. Why might elephants in the wild stand around a grave?

5. What "human" skills did the crow demonstrate when it used the wire to get food?

6. What might animal researchers say is the main difference between pets and wild animals?

Connect to the Big Question

After reading the article, how would you explain why animals help people in times of conflict?

Real-Life Connection

Have you ever shared a deep, personal secret with someone you trust? Were you afraid that the person you told would talk to other kids? Why or why not? What do you think of when you think about trust? Make a word web like the one below. Use it to write your thoughts.

What does it mean?

Why is it important?

Trust

How do you build it?

How do you lose it?

WORD BANK

argue (AHR gyoo) *verb*   To **argue** with someone is to disagree with the person in a discussion.
EXAMPLE: *Jamal did not want to argue with his parents, so he agreed to come home by nine o'clock.*

game (gaym) *noun*   A **game** is an activity with a winner that people do for fun or sport.
EXAMPLE: *My brother's favorite game is checkers, but everyone else I know prefers Monopoly.*

issue (I shoo) *noun*   An **issue** is an important problem people are working to solve.
EXAMPLE: *Littering is not as big an issue at my school now that we have a recycling program.*

resist (ri ZIST) *verb*   To **resist** something is to struggle against it.
EXAMPLE: *Marcus tried to resist playing with his dog, but he finally got up from his desk and threw a toy.*

search (suhrch) *verb*   When you **search** for something, you look carefully to try to find it.
EXAMPLE: *I will search my backpack and locker, but I am almost sure I left my book at home.*

Is conflict always bad?

Did you ever play the game "pin the tail on the donkey"? Did you trust the person who spun you around and told you where to go? If you missed the donkey, it was no big deal. Life, however, can be a lot riskier than a game. As you read the article, ask yourself: **Can fear be replaced with trust?**

Building Trust and Replacing Fear

You stand with a group of teenagers on a high rock overlooking a pond. It is a hot summer day. Everyone wants to cool off. One boy jumps in. He comes to the surface and tells the others to jump. You have never been there. You do not know how deep the pond is. You do not know if there are rocks beneath the dark surface. You want to get cool. You want to be cool.

"The water's great!" the boy says. "Jump!"

In a situation like that, you probably do not want to **argue** with the person telling you to trust him or her. Still, it is natural to **resist** the urge to jump into unfamiliar water.

You do not stand at the edge of a cliff every day. However, you have probably experienced many times when you had to decide whether to trust other people. Such times come often in school. You may be asked to jump into a class discussion, tryouts for a team, or a role in a play. If you do not trust your peers, fear will win. In schools where trust among students is low, kids can become isolated. This lack of trust can create problems for a school. Bullying, poor grades, and substance abuse can make school a frightening place.

▲ **If you had to climb a wall, who would you want on your team?**

WORKSHOPS TO BUILD TRUST Some schools have begun **searching** for ways to help students build trust in one another. They have turned to trust-building workshops. These workshops may take place in school or in another place set aside for them.

In these workshops, students and some adults hold discussions about an **issue**, such as bullying, that may affect the school. They play **games** that force the students to work as teammates. The students have to **search** for ways to make everyone feel comfortable.

> Some schools have begun to search for ways to help students build trust.

Some workshops that are held away from school use physical challenges to build trust. One program in Virginia, called Hemlock Overlook, has students step onto a platform 40 feet above the ground. Students have to trust their classmates to hold the platform steady. Kids prove that they will not let one another get hurt physically. Then they can trust that they will not hurt one another emotionally. "It's a little bit *Survivor* and a little bit *Fear Factor*," says the assistant director of Hemlock Overlook.

A program called Challenge Day holds workshops in schools across the United States. The workshops address important **issues** that cause fear. The **issues** may include relationships, bullying, academics, loneliness, and substance abuse. Such workshops challenge students to make one positive change every day. A student who went to a Challenge Day workshop said, "I felt lonely and isolated for most of my middle school years." She is now a youth leader and tutor for younger children.

DO WORKSHOPS REALLY WORK? Some people are **resistant** to trust-building workshops. They say that one day spent playing games will not work. Learning to trust people takes much longer.

Other critics say that too few students take part in the activities. In some cases, no more than a hundred students can take part. Workshops should include everyone, say the critics.

Critics also point out that there is no way to measure the success of the workshops. Replacing fear with trust cannot be measured on a test. Some students might say that they feel more trusting. Others might have learned to be kinder to their classmates. However, the **issues** and **arguments** that affect a school may remain.

MORE FOLLOW-UP Many workshop leaders agree that follow-up is needed. One day cannot solve all the problems. One workshop cannot change a person forever. However, it can be a strong beginning. Many students who have attended say they have experienced a change in attitude. They believe it is worth one day of their lives to start a process that could last longer.

It may not be possible for every young person to replace fear with trust. Some people may not be able to change. However, if one young person learns to trust, that feeling can spread like ripples in a pond.

"Instead of being competitive and working against each other, [workshops are] cooperative, with everybody helping each other," says the director of Hemlock Overlook.

WRAP IT UP

Find It on the Page

1. Where do trust-building workshops take place?

2. Briefly summarize objections to trust-building workshops.

Use Clues

3. What does standing on a high platform have to do with creating a trusting school atmosphere?

4. What advice would you give to schools that want to reduce students' feelings of loneliness and isolation?

5. What is your opinion of trust-building workshops? Why?

Connect to the Big Question

After reading the article, do you think fear can be replaced with trust? How?

Real-Life Connection

Copy the chart below. Take a moment to preview the text by looking at subheads and photos. Then write a prediction of what the article will be about.

Heading	Prediction
Title: A Winner On and Off the Field	
Subhead 1:	
Subhead 2:	

Check It Out

Resilience (ri ZIL yuhns) is the ability to recover and heal after things go wrong. Here are three qualities that help people be resilient:

- They know the difference between right and wrong.
- They have fun to let out stress.
- They know where to turn for help.

battle (BA tuhl) *noun*   A **battle** is a fight or struggle.
  EXAMPLE: *Ed loves watching teams **battle** to win the World Series.*

class (klas) *noun*   A **class** is a group of students who meet with a teacher regularly to study the same subject.
  EXAMPLE: *Ms. Song's writing **class** is interviewing athletes.*

game (gaym) *noun*   A **game** is an activity with a winner that people do for fun or sport.
  EXAMPLE: *Our baseball team plays at least one **game** a week.*

resolve (ri ZAHLV) *verb*   To **resolve** something is to find an answer or a solution to it.
  EXAMPLE: *Joe had to **resolve** his fears before going rock climbing.*

win (win) *verb*   When you **win** something, you beat another person or team in a contest or you reach your goal.
  EXAMPLE: *If we **win** today's game, we will go to the semifinals.*

THE BIG ?

Is conflict always bad?

A little boy suffers through his parents' divorce. His father moves away and his mother has to work all the time. Despite these challenges, he grows up to be a star athlete. He also becomes a happy and well-adjusted adult. As you read the article, ask yourself: **Can conflict build character?**

A Winner On and Off the Field

Blink your eyes. That is how much time a major-league ballplayer has to decide whether to swing at a pitch. Alex Rodriguez has made the right decision more than 500 times. That is how many home runs he has hit in his career. In 2007, Rodriguez hit two home runs in *one inning* for the New York Yankees. His teammate, Derek Jeter, said Rodriguez "makes [hitting] look easy—and it's not easy."

Baseball may seem easy to Rodriguez—or A-Rod, as he is known. He played his first big-league game at age eighteen. He is the youngest player to hit 500 home runs in his career, and for his skills he is paid about $25 million a year. However, as good as life may be for A-Rod now, growing up was a **battle**.

CHILDHOOD CHALLENGES Rodriguez was born in New York City in 1975. His parents were from the Dominican Republic. When Rodriquez was four years old, his family moved back there. That is where he first played baseball. When he was seven, the family returned to the United States and moved to Miami, Florida. Soon afterward, Rodriguez's parents divorced, and his dad moved away.

▲ Alex Rodriguez batting for the New York Yankees

Rodriguez's mother worked two jobs to support Alex and his sister and brother. Her struggle led him to **resolve** to become a professional baseball player so his mother would not have to work.

Because Rodriguez's mother was at work most days, he spent much of his free time at the Boys and Girls Clubs of Miami. There, he developed his natural skills and became a talented baseball player in high school. He worked hard in **class** and on the baseball field. He led his high school team to **win** the national championship. A year later, he was playing in the big leagues.

Because of Rodriguez's success, his mother will never have to work again. He also made a **resolution** to help young people **battling** difficulties. He started the Alex Rodriguez Learning Center in Miami to help kids build reading, math, and computer skills.

▲ **Alex Rodriguez works hard for what he believes in both on and off the field.**

TOUGH TIMES NOT OVER What is the main reason for Alex Rodriguez's success? Many believe it is his resiliency. When he overcame the challenges of childhood, he realized that he could overcome other challenges that life threw at him.

"Kids who have experienced tough times are actually stronger adults," says one expert. "They've learned that no matter what happens, they can handle it!"

Although Rodriguez makes millions playing baseball, he still faces tough times. For three years, he played for the New York Yankees, one of the most successful teams in baseball history. When A-Rod joined the team in 2004, fans expected him to lead the Yankees to the World Series. He did not make that happen.

Yankee fans were disappointed. They said that any player who makes $25 million a year should lead his team to a championship. Fans booed him when he failed to get a key hit in a **game.**

However, A-Rod is not giving up. He believes that the lessons he learned growing up have helped him during his tough times as a ballplayer. He knows that nothing he faces as an adult can compare to the challenges he faced growing up poor in Miami. Rodriguez gives his mother credit for helping him **win** out over his childhood problems. She always supported him, whether he won or lost.

Rodriguez does not just talk about his life. He also writes about it. In 1998 he wrote a book for young people called *Hit a Grand Slam!* It tells the story of his life, including his **battles** to overcome challenges. It also gives advice on how young people can achieve their goals.

A-Rod has **won** more than baseball **games.** He has **won** the respect of his peers in baseball and in his community—and he has the love of a strong family. Compared with these things, **winning** a World Series can seem unimportant.

WRAP IT UP

Find It on the Page

1. Where did Alex Rodriguez spend most of his childhood?

2. What challenges did he face growing up?

3. Summarize the information on Alex's childhood.

Use Clues

4. How can you tell that Alex has not forgotten his tough times growing up?

5. In your opinion, why did fans take out their unhappiness with a team on a player as good as A-Rod?

6. How can facing challenges in childhood help people face challenges in adulthood?

Connect to the Big Question

After reading the article, would you say that conflict can build character? Why or why not?

Real-Life Connection

Have you ever heard of pop culture? What do you know about pop culture in countries around the world? Take a moment to write down what you know about famous people and popular activities around the world.

Check It Out

A *culture* is made up of the normal parts of everyday life shared by a group of people in a certain place or time.

- *Culture* includes religious beliefs and values, ethnic and social background, and even food, clothing, and entertainment choices.
- Popular culture, also called pop culture, refers to parts of a culture well known and accepted by most people in the culture.

WORD BANK

clue (kloo) *noun*   A **clue** is a piece of information that helps you find an answer.
EXAMPLE: *The crumbs on Joe were a **clue** that he had eaten the cake.*

compete (kuhm PEET) *verb*   When you **compete,** you try to win against someone else.
EXAMPLE: *We will **compete** against Greensburg in the final game.*

conclude (kuhn KLOOD) *verb*   You **conclude** something when you make a decision using the available information.
EXAMPLE: *The long silence on the other end of the phone helped me **conclude** that my friend had fallen asleep!*

convince (kuhn VINS) *verb*   You **convince** people of something when you get them to agree with you.
EXAMPLE: *I am trying to **convince** my parents that my music sounds better when it is loud.*

survival (suhr VY vuhl) *noun*   **Survival** means staying alive in difficult situations.
EXAMPLE: *An oil spill can threaten the **survival** of sea birds.*

Is conflict always bad?

You can read about them in magazines, you can see them on TV, and it seems that everyone talks about them. Who are they? They are pop icons, people most of us recognize. Why are they so important to so many of us? As you read the article, ask yourself: **What do pop icons tell us about a culture?**

World Pop Cultures

Even if you do not like sports, you may know who Serena Williams is. If you have never seen a movie with Brad Pitt, you still might recognize his face on a magazine cover. You probably cannot **convince** your parents to listen to your music. Even so, they might know who the musicians are. How do moms and dads know? The musicians might be pop icons. Pop icons are known to most people in a culture.

The pop icons mentioned above are from the United States. Have you ever wondered what athletes, actors, musicians, and artists are popular in other places? Some of these people are so popular, you may already have a **clue** who they are. Some pop icons are known all over the world.

POP ICONS CROSS CULTURES The United States is known for its pop culture. People who live in faraway countries may know American movie stars and sports heroes. Countries around the world have their own pop cultures. Some things we think of as American are not! The popular show *American Idol*, for example, started as a hit show in Great Britain. Eventually, it led to a similar show in Lebanon. Singers from all over the Middle East **compete** to win on *Star Academy*.

Animé is a very popular style ▶
of cartoon from Japan.

In most of the world, soccer is as big as football is in the United States. Soccer star Diego Maradona is as famous in Argentina as football star Peyton Manning is in the United States. In fact, soccer is the most watched **competitive** sport on earth.

Soccer is the world's most popular sport.

We think of Hollywood as the movie center of the world. Moviemaking, however, is thriving in other parts of the world. Jackie Chan made many movies for Asian audiences before he made it big in the United States. In India, you will find Bollywood—a name formed by replacing the *H* in *Hollywood* with the *B* in *Bombay* (the old name for the city Mumbai). There, Indian actors make Hollywood-scale blockbusters.

Music from around the world has something for everyone. "Music is universal. To discover the music of a culture is to discover the culture as a whole," says critic Megan Romer. Singer Manu Chao was born in Spain and raised in France. He sings in seven languages. Everything from punk rock to reggae to salsa to Paris café music appears on his CDs. Habib Koite is from Mali, a country in West Africa. He fuses traditional Malian music with American influences. One of his favorite performers is Usher.

Japan has a **convincing** lead in creating a cartoon style called animé (AN uh may). About 60 percent of all the cartoons watched around the world today come from Japan. Animé started in the 1970s with hits like *Pokemon* and *Sailor Moon*. "Japanimation" has become the world's favorite form of animation.

WILL CULTURES CONFLICT? The blending of cultures brings people around the world closer together. Are these cultural influences good or bad? Some people argue that the "popular" in American popular culture is bad for other countries' identities. They fear that traditions around the world will not **survive.** In one poll, 70 percent of Americans said they believed U.S. pop culture had a big impact on the world. Nearly 50 percent of people polled said they thought that impact was negative. However, almost 70 percent of those polled approved of new ideas and cultural influences coming into the United States from other countries. They thought that sampling other cultures could help Americans understand other nations.

Some studies **conclude** that the spread of U.S. pop culture could help breath life into traditional cultures. People in Africa, Asia, Latin America, and the Caribbean take U.S. cultural forms and change them by mixing them with local traditions. Conflict between a pop culture and a traditional culture can actually result in both the **survival** of the traditional culture and a creative move forward.

Wherever you live, you can tap into pop cultures from around the world. You can listen to the same music as your cousin in Haiti. You can watch the World Cup soccer finals or the latest animé. You can enjoy more variety from more cultures than any generation before yours.

WRAP IT UP

Find It on the Page

1. Where did the idea for *American Idol* come from?

2. What is the world's most watched sport?

3. List two points from the article about blending cultures.

Use Clues

4. How might access to different cultures be good for relations between different countries?

5. What advice would you give to someone trying to learn about a new culture?

6. Do you think that the blending of cultures strengthens them or weakens them? Why?

Connect to the Big Question

After reading the article, what do you think pop icons tell us about a given culture?

Real-Life Connection

One thing all heroes have in common is that they make an uncommon choice. Heroes do the thing that most of us would not. What do you think of when you hear the word *hero?* Make a word web like the one below. Use it to jot down your ideas.

What they say

What they do

Heroes

What they look like

What others say about them

WORD BANK

defend (di FEND) *verb*   To **defend** is to protect someone or something from danger.
EXAMPLE: *Our basketball team is playing to **defend** the trophy we won last year.*

discover (dis KUH vuhr) *verb*   To **discover** something is to see it or understand it for the first time.
EXAMPLE: *Sometimes reading a good book can help you **discover** something true about yourself.*

issue (I shoo) *noun*   An **issue** is an important problem people are working to solve.
EXAMPLE: *The city council is voting on the **issue** of teen curfews.*

negotiate (ni GOH shee ayt) *verb*   You **negotiate** when you talk with someone else to solve a problem through give and take.
EXAMPLE: *Jared and I are trying to **negotiate** who will get the gym ready for the football rally.*

resist (ri ZIST) *verb*   To **resist** something is to struggle against it.
EXAMPLE: *I tried to **resist** the french fries, but finally I just gave in and ate them.*

Is conflict always bad?

When you think of a hero, what do you picture? You might imagine anything from a soldier to a superhero. You probably do not picture a person your own age. The truth is, people of all ages do amazing things every day. As you read the article, ask yourself: **What can we learn from kids who become heroes?**

What Makes a Hero?

Stephanie Shearman was running in a 5K fun race when she became a hero. She was trying to **defend** her lead over a father and daughter, but they passed her. Suddenly she heard the daughter scream. When she caught up, the father was on the ground, turning purple. The daughter yelled, "Does anybody here know CPR?" Nobody answered. Maybe no one knew CPR. More likely, the bystanders just froze. People often **resist** taking charge in an emergency. Shearman had to **negotiate** with herself to make the right choice. "I was the only kid there, and I didn't want to look stupid," Shearman explains. "But when she asked again, I went right over and got started."

Shearman performed CPR till help came. The man was rushed to a hospital. Thanks to Shearman's quick thinking, he survived. "I wouldn't say that I feel like a hero," she says. "But I felt pretty grateful that I knew what to do. I think everyone should know CPR."

When we think of heroes, we do not usually think of young people like Shearman. The fact, though, is that you do not have to be a certain age to be a hero. You just have to have certain qualities.

HELP!

▲ **What would you do in an emergency?**

RISKING THEIR LIVES TO SAVE OTHERS Many kids have saved lives. Some kids have even risked their own lives to do so. Eleven-year-old Michelle saved two people from drowning. She managed to do that even though she could not swim. After the plane Tammy was on crashed, the six-year-old **resisted** giving up. She dragged her badly injured sister several miles through the woods to find help. The father of seventeen-year-old Andrew fell off a boat. The propeller nearly cut off the father's leg. Andrew found the strength to pull him out of the water.

What was it about these kids that made them go forward in the face of danger? When the pressure was on, each of them made a quick decision. They chose to put helping another person ahead of their own safety. Some heroes have to react in a split second. Others fight danger and hardship over a long time.

FIGHTING LONG BATTLES Saca was so badly scalded as a baby that she lost both legs. Pain was her battlefield. Saca made the decision to focus her energy. By age fourteen, she had become the fourth fastest wheelchair racer in the world.

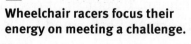

Wheelchair racers focus their energy on meeting a challenge.

A group called Brave Kids provides resources for children with life-threatening illnesses. Some of these kids face chemotherapy, which makes them feel sick and exhausted for months at a time. Some face frustration to relearn how to use damaged arms or legs. Some **discover** the incredible pain of having burn wounds cleaned every day for months. The **issue** for these kids is not saving someone else's life, but saving their own. These kids do not give up. They make the choice many of us would not. Day after day, they choose to fight for survival. Every day is a **negotiation** with pain.

DIFFERENT KINDS OF COURAGE Which takes more courage—reacting in a split second to save someone's life or coping with suffering for months or years? Is it more heroic to take a risk that you did not expect or to face a problem every day that you know is waiting for you?

Some people say that those who risk their lives for others are more foolish than brave. Two lives are now at risk instead of one. Others say that rescuing is an instinct, not a choice. For most of us, it is natural to show **resistance** to facing danger. In some cases, though, a person is driven to act anyway. Still others think that sacrificing oneself is the bravest thing one can do.

Neal Shusterman is the author of *Kid Heroes: True Stories of Rescuers, Survivors, and Achievers*. "Heroes come in all shapes and sizes," he says. He believes that all these kids are heroes—the kids who save lives, and the kids who fight their way through hardships and disabilities. All these young people have one thing in common: They all made positive choices in negative circumstances.

WRAP IT UP

Find It on the Page

1. How did Stephanie Shearman save a man's life?

2. What did six-year-old Tammy do that was heroic?

3. Briefly summarize what the group Brave Kids does.

Use Clues

4. Compare and contrast the two types of courage discussed in this article.

5. Of the two types of courage, which do you think is more difficult? Why?

6. Is there any way to prepare yourself to be a hero? Explain.

Connect to the Big Question

After reading the article, what do you think we can learn from kids who resist danger and hardship and become heroes?

Real-Life Connection

Krumping (KRUHM ping) is a type of urban dance. What do you know about krumping? Fill out a knowledge rating chart like the one below to find out.

Idea	Know a Lot	Know a Little	Know Nothing
What krumping looks like			
What the purpose of krumping is			
Where krumping started			

Check It Out

Krumping involves moves that are very fast and very physical. It often involves competing with other dancers. Many krumpers see it as a safe alternative to street life. In the dance, they can be aggressive without being violent. The dancers in a crew are like family. They help each other out with krumping and other areas of life, too.

WORD BANK

battle (BA tuhl) *noun*   A **battle** is a fight or struggle.
   EXAMPLE: *Will Dragon **battle** with Milk for the top krump spot?*

challenge (CHA luhnj) *noun*   A **challenge** is a difficult situation to deal with.
   EXAMPLE: *It can be a **challenge** to focus on school when you are surrounded by other choices.*

convince (kuhn VINS) *verb*   You **convince** people of something when you get them to agree with you.
   EXAMPLE: *Yael tried to **convince** Suze that he was a better dancer.*

perform (puhr FAWRM) *verb*   To **perform** is to do something that requires special skills, in front of an audience.
   EXAMPLE: *Giselle agreed to **perform** the dance even though she was nervous about the large crowd.*

win (win) *verb*   When you **win** something, you beat another person or team in a contest or you reach your goal.
   EXAMPLE: *Whether we **win** or lose the game, we are still a team.*

Is conflict always bad?

Some kids are standing in a circle, listening to hip-hop music. One boy goes to the center. He starts dancing fast and furiously. What is going on? It is a krumping contest. As you read the article, ask yourself: **Can competitions like krumping provide an alternative to street life?**

Krumping Contests: Battles Where Nobody Gets Hurt

Do you krump? Krumping is a style of dance that is not much older than you. It is all about energy and self-expression—and competition. It has been called extreme hip-hop.

THE CREATION OF KRUMP There is some debate about how krumping got started. Most experts agree that it began in 1992 in South Central Los Angeles. A man named Tommy Johnson would **perform** as Tommy the Clown at kids' parties. He began adding dance moves to his **performance.** Eventually, he had a crew of young clown dancers. Soon, other crews appeared to **challenge** Johnson and his kids. He started the **Battle** Zone, a contest in which dancers compete and the audience decides who **wins.**

Battle Zone competitions take place in huge stadiums with thousands of audience members. The same dancers may face off against each other week after week. As a result, exciting rivalries develop. The **winners** are rewarded with giant belts like those given out in professional wrestling. Talented **performers** gain the respect of their communities and peers.

Some of Johnson's clowns left to form their own dance group, the Krump Kings.

A next-generation krumper practices his moves.

They say they took clown dancing to the next level—krumping. Johnson says *he* did. Either way, krumping just keeps getting bigger. It has spread to Europe and Asia. Famous musicians like Missy Elliott, Outkast, and the Black Eyed Peas have used it in their videos. It has even been featured on the TV show *So You Think You Can Dance.*

Krumping appeals to a lot of different people. It has room for dancers who like to use different styles. It has room for people who wear clown makeup and for those who prefer African-inspired war paint. Either way, the face paint acts as a mask. It allows the dancers to create new identities. Tommy Johnson calls his face paint his "weapon" and dancing his "getaway." Dancers also give themselves new names, like Lil' C, Tight Eyez, and Miss Prissy.

Move	Description
Popping	Made by flexing muscles and joints to the beat. Uses elements of mime.
Spins	Turns down on an isolated body part (heads, knees, shoulders), often inverted and begun by the hands, feet, or angle of the torso.
Top rock	An upright form of dancing. Usually a string of steps used to open a dance.
Uprock	A "dancing fight" performed with quick, continuous movement. Dancers are very close to each other but don't actually touch.
Robot precise	Isolated movements and turns that lock into place before the next movement begins.

SOME KRUMPING MOVES

Information is from PureMovement's Hip Hop Study Guide.

A famous photographer made a movie about krumping called *Rize.* It came out in 2005. It intercuts scenes of krumpers **battling** each other with scenes of dancers in Africa. Even though the American dancers had never seen traditional African dances, the dancers came up with similar moves and used similar makeup. The similarities are truly amazing.

AN ALTERNATIVE TO VIOLENCE One thing Tommy Johnson and the Krump Kings agree on is that krumping gives young people a creative outlet. It also helps keep them out of gangs and other trouble. It gives them something physically and emotionally healthy to do outside of school hours. It gives dancers a positive way to express their frustration and anger. It is a **challenge** they can face with their crew and that they can have fun doing. Tommy Johnson says, "It is a very positive thing, because it really does keep kids off the streets."

The dancers are **convinced** that violence is not the answer to their problems. They release pent-up aggression in the dance. They face their demons. One dancer says, "This is our ghetto ballet." The dancers also disagree with the way some commercial hip-hop makes ghetto life look glamorous. Krumpers may have friends and family members who are involved with gangs and drugs. They have seen up close that there is nothing glamorous about that way of life. For them, krumping is an escape from it all.

Krumping is becoming more and more popular. It happens everywhere from auditoriums to the street. Krumpers meet in parking lots, playgrounds, and yards to **battle** dance. Many people hope krumpers will convert other people to antidrug, nonviolent values.

WRAP IT UP

Find It on the Page

1. When and where did krumping begin?

2. In what settings does krumping take place?

3. In your own words, explain two moves from the chart.

4. What is the main thing that krumpers are against? Explain.

5. In what way is conflict a good thing when it comes to krumping?

6. What might be a better way to learn about dance and music than words on a page? Why?

Connect to the Big Question

After reading the article, do you think competitions like krumping can provide an alternative to street life? Why or why not?

 **Debate**

 Answer the Big Question: Is conflict always bad?
You have read about different conflicts and ways in which people handle conflict. Now, use what you learned to answer the Unit 2 Big Question (BQ).

STEP 1: Form a Group and Choose
Your first step is to pick Unit 2 articles that you like.
Get together. Find a small group to work with.
Read the list of articles. Discuss which articles listed on the left side of this page were the most interesting to you.
Choose two or more articles. Pick articles that you all agree on.

STEP 2: Reread and Answer the Unit Big Question
Your next step is to begin forming your viewpoint for a debate.
Reread the articles you chose. As you reread, think about the Unit BQ.
Answer questions. For each article you chose, answer these questions:
- What conflict is the article about?
- Is the conflict solved? If so, how? If not, why not?
- How would you answer the Unit BQ: Is conflict always bad?

Form groups. Divide your small group into two teams. One team will present the viewpoint *Yes, conflict is always bad.* The other team will present *No, conflict is not always bad.*

STEP 3: Find Examples and Discuss Reasons
During this step, begin to develop your argument.
Find examples in the articles. Support your answer to the BQ by using examples from the articles you chose. Your examples should clearly support the idea that conflict is or is not always bad. Also, list supporting examples not from the articles.
Discuss your reasons. With your team, choose the strongest reasons for your view. Underline them to use in the debate.

STEP 4: Strengthen Your Argument

Now, finish your debate argument.

Choose the examples for your argument. Look over the examples and discuss which ones best support your argument. Underline the ones that are most convincing.

Talk about how to present your argument. Think about your audience. Which reasons do you think they will find the most convincing?

Put your reasons in order. You might start with the least convincing reason and end with the best. This leaves a strong impression with your audience.

STEP 5: Strengthen Your Work

Next, you and your team will discuss your debating points to be sure that you have a convincing argument.

Use the rubric. Use the questions in the rubric to evaluate your work. Answer each question yes or no.

Discuss your evaluations. If you have yes answers, can you make those debating points even stronger? If you have any no answers, what can you do to change your argument before you present it?

Improve your argument. Look over your reasons again to be sure that you have chosen convincing ones. Improve your argument before you present it to the class.

STEP 6: Practice and Present

Get ready to practice and present your debate.

Practice what you want to say. Divide the debating points among your team members. Be sure that you have your reasons in order from least convincing to most convincing. You want to leave a strong impression with your audience.

Present your viewpoint. Present your side of the debate, and the other team will present theirs. You might take turns with the other team—each member of each team presenting a reason and giving examples to support it.

UNIT 3

What is important to know?

If you are lost, what is important to know? It is important to know directions! What else do you think is important to know? In this unit, you will read about topics from justice to body language to wilderness survival. As you read, think about the Big Question and ask yourself: What is important to know?

What is the most important thing that you have learned? How did you learn it? Why was this so important to know?

Real-Life Connection

Is it possible to communicate without words? What do you know about body language? The following chart gives examples of ways our bodies might send a message. In a similar chart, write what message you think each gesture sends. There may be more than one answer.

Body Position	Possible Message
Crossed arms on chest	*I am relaxed or upset.*
Hands on hips	
Arm raised with hand making fist	
Sitting with hands clasped behind head	

WORD BANK

distinguish (di STING wish) *verb*   To **distinguish** between two things means to tell the difference between them.
EXAMPLE: *It was difficult for me to **distinguish** the twins from each other.*

examine (ig ZA muhn) *verb*   To **examine** something is to look closely at it to learn facts.
EXAMPLE: *Hasan decided to **examine** the topic for his research paper by reading several books.*

imitate (I muh tayt) *verb*   You act the same as other people when you **imitate** them.
EXAMPLE: *José's little brothers often **imitate** the way he talks and walks.*

observe (uhb ZUHRV) *verb*   When you **observe** someone or something, you watch the person or thing carefully.
EXAMPLE: *The judges will **observe** each athlete's performance.*

purpose (PUHR puhs) *noun*   A **purpose** is the reason that something exists or is done.
EXAMPLE: *The **purpose** of this raffle is to raise money for Gina's trip to Africa.*

What is important to know?

Take a quick look around the room. Can you tell anything about people's moods just by looking at them? Maybe they are sending messages with their bodies. As you read the article, ask yourself: **Is body language a truer form of communication than using words?**

The Language of the Body

Imagine you are at a party. You start to cross the room to talk to a friend. Then you stop to **observe** him. He is leaning against a wall with his arms crossed. Is he sending you the message "Don't come near me"? Is your friend saying "I'm relaxed"? You say hello. He looks up and says a friendly hi, but he keeps his arms crossed. Now you are really confused.

Humans are better than any other animal at communicating, or sending and receiving messages. The messages can be verbal or nonverbal. Verbal messages are sent with words. The words can be spoken, written, or even signed with the hands. Nonverbal messages are sent without words. This second type of communication is called body language. Body language includes any movement we use that might send messages. Since we can perform so many movements, it is no wonder that body language can be so confusing.

EXTENT OF BODY LANGUAGE Some types of body language are deliberate. They are done with a **purpose.** For example, a friend chooses to point her finger at something to get you to notice it.

What message is this person sending with his body language? ▶

Other types of body language, like blushing or crying, are involuntary. An involuntary action is one the body does automatically.

People use many parts of their body to send nonverbal messages. **Examine** what the eyes alone can communicate. According to one body language expert, "Of all parts of the human body that are used to transmit information, the eyes are the most important." We use our eyes and the muscles around them to express emotions. We open our eyes wide when we are surprised. We squint when we doubt what we are hearing.

People use many movements to speak nonverbally. They nod their heads up and down to say yes. They shake

> **What does a person sitting up very straight say?**

them from side to side to say no. People raise their shoulders to say, "I don't know." They may even use their entire bodies to communicate. What does a person sitting up very straight say? Is it a different message if the person slouches at a desk?

DIFFERENCES IN BODY LANGUAGE A few types of body language are universal. This means they are used and understood by people in all parts of the world. One example of universal body language is a true smile. All humans express happiness by turning up the corners of their mouths for a few seconds. We also all reveal surprise, fear, anger, and strong dislike in similar ways.

Most body language, however, is not universal. This is because we learn nonverbal communication as children living in certain communities. As babies, we **imitate** the expressions and gestures of family members and other people around us. As adults, our body language matches that of the people we know.

There are differences in body language between countries and even age groups. In much of North America, a young person is expected to look at an older person's face during a conversation. In Latin America, this behavior would seem disrespectful. In the United States, young people are less likely to use formal handshakes than older people are. Through **observation,** you can learn to **distinguish** the meaning of one action or expression from that of another and avoid making mistakes. What might seem friendly in one culture could seem offensive in another.

HOW RELIABLE IS BODY LANGUAGE? Even among people who do use similar styles of body language, "reading" it can be tricky. What if a friend's body language does not match what she is saying? Which message do you believe, the verbal one or the nonverbal one?

Studies show that nonverbal communication can be truer than words, especially if it is an involuntary response. What if you misread it? Gestures and positions can have multiple meanings. (Remember how hard it was to "read" the guy at the party?) **Imitating** someone's body language can give you clues to what the person is feeling. In the end, though, it is up to you to decide what is true. Do more than listen to words. Carefully watch body language, too. Then decide what is really being said.

WRAP IT UP

Find It on the Page

1. List the two types of messages that humans send and receive.

2. What is body language?

3. Name at least four parts of the body that can be used in body language.

Use Clues

4. How might body language cause a communication problem between two people?

5. Which type of communication do you trust more—verbal or nonverbal? Explain.

6. What could you do to avoid making mistakes when trying to read body language?

Connect to the Big Question

After reading the article, which means of human communication do you think is more reliable— body language or words?

Real-Life Connection

Trying to balance school work with a job can be really hard. Would you take a part-time job or not? What kinds of things would you think about in making the choice? Copy the chart below to list the benefits and drawbacks to getting a job.

Benefits to getting a job	Drawbacks to getting a job

guess (ges) *verb*   When you **guess** something, you form an opinion of it without having all the information about it.
EXAMPLE: *Shana was so prepared for the quiz that she did not have to **guess** any of the answers.*

judge (juhj) *verb*   When you **judge,** you form an opinion or make a decision based on facts.
EXAMPLE: *Marcos always thinks people are older than they really are because he has never been able to **judge** age well.*

organize (AWR guh nyz) *verb*   When you **organize,** you put separate parts into some kind of order.
EXAMPLE: *We need to **organize** all of the magazines on this shelf by title.*

probably (PRAH buh blee) *adverb*   To say something will **probably** happen means you are pretty sure it will happen.
EXAMPLE: *Dwayne is really talented, and he will **probably** win the art competition.*

study (STUH dee) *noun*   Scientists conduct a **study** when they test an idea or research a subject.
EXAMPLE: *Mia's **study** showed that most of the kids in our class have after-school activities.*

What is important to know?

The busier you get, the harder it is to balance all the things in your life. A job brings in extra money, but school helps you get ready for your future. Can you do both? As you read the article, ask yourself: **Is it worth having a job while in school?**

Teens at Work

Beep! Beep! Beep! Your alarm clock wakes you up out of a sound sleep. You get up, rush to get ready, and spend the day in classes. There are sports teams and drama clubs and other activities to **organize** your time around. For most high school students, going to school is a full-time job. Why add a part-time job to all that school stress?

Some teenagers simply do not have a choice. Their families need the money. For other students, the main reason to work is to make money they can spend any way they want. Either way, a part-time job can teach important skills. It can also get in the way of school.

Many teens work and go to school. A University of Washington **study** showed that 56% of high school seniors had jobs during the school year. Can you **guess** what most teenagers spend that hard-earned money on? You **probably guessed** right: clothes, music, movies, cars, and food. So, is it a good idea to work and go to school? Unfortunately, there is no easy way to **judge** this choice.

THE VALUE OF A JOB Students who work are more likely to learn money skills. These students understand what it means to earn money. They learn how to use their money or save it in an account.

▲ **Many teens learn important work skills at after-school jobs.**

For many parents, having their teens spend their own money also helps the family with finances.

Working has other benefits, too. Teens become more confident when they do jobs well. They can learn to be responsible, because others rely on them. Teens can also gain important skills that they do not always learn in the classroom. They may learn how to solve problems in difficult situations or to deal with different types of people. Teens who work may learn important **organizational** skills. They must balance work with school and life.

Some working students experience feelings of stress and exhaustion.

A PRICE TO PAY? Some parents question whether having a job is the best thing for their teenager. Will it get in the way of schoolwork? Will a job interfere with sports or the arts? Will their teenager have to cut time for having fun and just being a teenager?

A **study** done by the University of California, Berkeley, showed that teens who worked more than 15 hours per week did not do as well in school as other teens. They did less homework and got lower grades. They were also more likely to drop out of school than the students who worked fewer hours.

Other **studies** have shown that students who work too many hours have more stress than other teens. These teens do not spend enough time doing the things they enjoy. They give up such activities in order to work and go to school. All people need time just to have fun and relax. Without it, stress can really pile up.

A HAPPY MEDIUM? One option that may balance work with school is a work-study program. In a work-study program, schools team up with local businesses. They work together to set up jobs for student workers. Students learn new skills. They get paid and earn school credit toward graduation. They also get to work with local business leaders and set goals.

Good work-study programs, however, can be hard to find. A researcher at the University of California thinks that a successful program "must be carefully planned and monitored by people who understand both the work setting and what is to be learned there." He believes that without the right people to organize the program, work-study probably will not work.

Should teens work or focus on school and other activities? Students who work may struggle both in and out of school. They may also gain important skills. Working students who **organize** their time for work, school, and having fun tend to be the most successful. In the end, the decision is personal. It is a **judgment** that must be made one student, and one worker, at a time.

WRAP IT UP

Find It on the Page

1. What percentage of high school seniors work during the school year?

2. What are three things teens can learn by working a part-time job?

3. Briefly summarize the possible drawbacks to students working.

Use Clues

4. Why can students who work too many hours have stress?

5. If you had to get a job, what kinds of things would you do to keep your life balanced?

6. Do you think a work-study job is better for students than a regular part-time job? Explain.

Connect to the Big Question

After reading the article, do you think it is a good idea to have a job while in school?

Real-Life Connection

During the civil rights movement, people fought racial injustice. Laws were created to protect the rights of all Americans, no matter what their race. When you hear the words *civil rights,* what do you think of? Make a word web like the one below to jot down your ideas.

Civil Rights

WORD BANK

demand (di MAND) *verb*   When you **demand** something, you ask for it as a right.
EXAMPLE: *The parents will **demand** a meeting with the principal.*

integrate (IN tuh grayt) *verb*   To **integrate** means to bring different parts together to make a whole.
EXAMPLE: *Our teacher plans to **integrate** vocabulary and reading in all his lessons.*

measure (ME zhuhr) *verb*   When you **measure** something, you find out its extent or size.
EXAMPLE: *Victor has to **measure** the height of the plants each day.*

narrow (NER oh) *adjective*   If you are **narrow** in thinking or choosing, you have a hard time being open to new ideas.
EXAMPLE: *You need to be more open-minded about this topic because your opinions on it are very **narrow.***

purpose (PUHR puhs) *noun*   A **purpose** is the reason that something exists or is done.
EXAMPLE: *The club's **purpose** is to help the community.*

What is important to know?

You know that less racial injustice exists in the United States today than in the past. Incidents of racial injustice still occur, though. What is being done about racial injustice today? As you read the article, ask yourself: How are today's young people continuing the struggle for racial justice?

Young People with Hope

The 1960s was a powerful time in the fight against racial injustice. There were sit-in protests at whites-only lunch counters. Cesar Chavez organized Latino farm workers to **demand** better working conditions. Martin Luther King, Jr., led more than 250,000 people in a march on Washington, D.C. There he gave his famous "I have a dream" speech. Soon after the march, President Lyndon B. Johnson signed the Civil Rights Act. One major **purpose** of this act was to **integrate** public places. Many great steps forward were made in the 1960s. These steps helped eliminate—or at least reduce—racial injustice.

Fast-forward to the present. What are things like today? Over the last forty years, has racial injustice finally died out? Unfortunately, the answer is no.

THE PRESENT SITUATION In 2006, the National Conference for Community and Justice (NCCJ) published an important survey. This survey was a **measure** of Americans' feelings about intergroup relations. Intergroup relations are the relationships between different groups of people. The groups can differ for racial, ethnic, social, or religious reasons. The NCCJ had published a similar survey in 2000.

The March on Washington in 1963

Comparing the two surveys showed some promising changes. Survey **measurements** showed increased contact between most groups. They also showed that racial and ethnic groups felt closer to one another than they had. Some of the new findings, however, were not so promising:

- Of the people surveyed, 75 percent felt that tension between groups was a "very serious or somewhat serious problem."
- Many Americans still saw themselves as treated unfairly "based on race or ethnicity" (32 percent of African Americans, 22.5 percent of Asians, 21 percent of Latinos, 9.5 percent of whites).

> In 1990, Hope Street Youth Development opened its doors in Wichita, Kansas.

Even though we have made great changes, people obviously still see racial injustice. Fortunately, dedicated groups of people continue to struggle against it. Not all of those people are adults.

A THING CALLED HOPE In 1990, Hope Street Youth Development opened its doors in Wichita, Kansas. The organization's **purpose** was to help middle school students with their schoolwork. Over the years, though, Hope Street expanded its mission. Anyone in fourth through twelfth grade could go there. Members got involved in community service projects. They started to make their voices heard, especially in the fight against **narrow** thinking.

One of their successes involved tackling racial injustice head-on. It started with a kid's expressing his frustration over being suspended from school. Some Hope Street members decided to study suspensions in Wichita schools. Here is what they discovered about the 2001–2002 school year:

- Minority students, 49 percent of the school population, received 65 percent of suspensions.
- African American students in particular, 23 percent of the school population, received almost 50 percent of suspensions.

Then the Hope Street members asked some serious questions: Why were minority students, especially African Americans, getting kicked out more often than other students? Did a link exist between the suspension rate and low grades? They wondered, how could kids be expected to learn if they were not even in school?

The Hope Street members decided to do something. They wrote a report on what they discovered. They also wrote recommendations for fixing the problem. The report, recommendations, and many meetings led the Wichita school system to adopt new **measures.** As a result, things began to change, and more students stayed in the classroom.

At Hope Street, young people have learned they can make a difference in their own lives and in their communities. One member says **purposefully,** "I always thought I could never change anything. I used to complain and complain. Since I joined Hope Street, I can create change on my own."

WRAP IT UP

Find It on the Page

1. Name two major events of the 1960s that took place in an effort to end racial injustice.

2. In what ways did Hope Street expand from its original mission?

3. Briefly summarize the actions of the Hope Street members on the issue of school suspensions.

Use Clues

4. What conclusion could you draw from the 2006 NCCJ survey?

5. Do you see people fighting racial injustice in the media or in your own life? Explain.

6. How would you recommend that people your age fight racial injustice?

Connect to the Big Question

Explain why and how young people today are continuing to fight for racial justice.

Real-Life Connection

In North America, professional baseball is run by a group called Major League Baseball (MLB). Some people think this group is more interested in making money than in the sport of baseball. Why might some people agree with this opinion and others disagree? Take a moment to write your thoughts on your own paper.

Check It Out

To understand the business side of baseball, take a look at these terms:

- *Commercialism* (kuh MUHR shuh li zuhm) refers to business deals in which the main point is to make money. It is often used negatively to describe making money at the cost of something personal.

- A *profit* (PRAH fuht) is the amount of money you make in business.

WORD BANK

establish (i STA blish) *verb*   You **establish** something when you put it in place or create it.
EXAMPLE: *We should **establish** some rules for this game before we start playing.*

question (KWES chuhn) *noun*   A **question** is something that is asked.
EXAMPLE: *Rochelle has a **question** she needs answered about the science competition.*

refer (ri FUHR) *verb*   To **refer** to something is to direct attention to it.
EXAMPLE: *Evan's friends usually **refer** to him as an example of a great team player.*

source (sawrs) *noun*   A **source** is a person, place, or thing that supplies something.
EXAMPLE: *That Web site was a good **source** of information about extreme sports.*

support (suh PAWRT) *verb*   To **support** something is to show that it is true, to be in favor of it, or to help it succeed.
EXAMPLE: *The facts in this article **support** what you told me about baseball history.*

What is important to know?

When you see a Major League Baseball game, you watch the players and their skills. You also see a lot of advertising. What do you think about all the moneymaking going on before and during the game? As you read the article, ask yourself: **Is big-league baseball too commercial?**

Major League Baseball and Money

Big-league baseball fans at a stadium see more than a ball game. They see advertisements posted everywhere. Ads are behind home plate, on the dugouts, and on the scoreboard. Fans watching the game on TV see even more ads. They see them not just during commercials, but during the actual game. They see close-ups of company logos. They hear that a bank has sponsored the batting order.

▲ Looking out on the field can mean seeing more than a ball game.

Some fans ask this **question:** Is Major League Baseball (MLB) more concerned about the sport of baseball or about making money? These fans feel that big-league baseball used to be played mostly for the love of the game. Is baseball really more commercial now than it used to be?

THE BUSINESS SIDE OF MLB Some fans think the early days of baseball had little to do with money. This is not true. Does the name William Wrigley, Jr., sound familiar? It probably does, and for two reasons: gum and baseball.

Wrigley made a fortune selling chewing gum and bought the Chicago Cubs in 1920. He used that money to **establish** the Cubs' ballpark, Wrigley Field. Think about baseball parks you know. Are they named after people, companies, or both? Some fans dislike the naming of ballparks after companies. They think it takes the personal feeling out of baseball. Others think it does not matter at all.

Once baseball became a professional sport, the players wanted to make money, too. After all, baseball was their job. Since the late 1960s, players have staged several strikes against MLB over money. One strike caused the 1994 World Series to be canceled.

MLB has always been about business. It is a for-profit organization. MLB makes money three ways. One **source** is ticket sales. Another is sales at stadiums of things like ad space, refreshments, and souvenirs. MLB also makes money—lots of it—from the broadcasting of games. Broadcasters like radio and TV stations pay MLB to air the games. **Refer** to the graph. It shows TV revenue, or income, for MLB over thirty years.

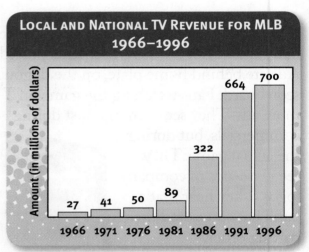

Information is from *The Economic History of Major League Baseball* by Michael J. Haupert.

ARE FAN COMPLAINTS REASONABLE? A baseball writer speaks for some fans when he says, "Instead of chasing dollars as a means to draw more fans, [MLB] should take the more profitable strategy of chasing fans as a means to earn dollars."

Some fans complain about rising ticket prices, players' huge salaries, and all the ads. At times, fans have done more than complain. They have acted. In 1999 and 2004, MLB was considering placing ads on players' uniforms. The group also made plans to place ads for an upcoming movie on bases. When fans protested loudly, however, all these plans were dropped.

Some sports analysts find fans' complaints **questionable.** These analysts argue that all professional sports have a lot of commercialism. Think of the money made from one Super Bowl ad. The analysts point out that NASCAR drivers' uniforms and cars are covered with ads. The analysts make **reference** to salaries of stars that exceed baseball players' salaries. They stress that baseball is, after all, a business. Businesses try to make money.

Yet, other sports analysts see things differently. These analysts use a number—13 percent—to **support** complaints about commercialism. In a 2006 poll, only 13 percent of Americans said that baseball was their favorite sport. Football and basketball each ranked higher than the "national pastime." These analysts argue that making baseball less commercial would help its popularity.

Whether or not you feel baseball is too commercial, one thing is certain: People love the game. While some fans may feel frustrated by ads and big business, they still hold their breath at every stolen base and cheer at every homerun.

WRAP IT UP

Find It on the Page

1. What is the connection between baseball and chewing gum?

2. What did money have to do with the 1994 World Series?

3. Name three sources of revenue for the owners of MLB teams.

Use Clues

4. Name one conclusion that can be drawn from the the graph.

5. Name two ways MLB could reduce commercialism that would please people your age.

6. Why do people disagree over whether big-league baseball is too commercial?

Connect to the Big Question

Do you think big-league baseball is too commercial? Support your answer.

Real-Life Connection

What do you know about wild birds that live in cities? Use a chart like the one below to check your knowledge. Put an *X* in the appropriate spaces.

Idea	Know a Lot	Know a Little	Know Nothing
How birds benefit humans			
Why urban areas are dangerous places for birds			
How people try to help urban birds			

Check It Out

Read on to learn some facts about birds.
- A predator (PRE duh tuhr) catches, kills, and eats other animals.
- Birds that migrate (MY grayt) move from one region to another because of the changing seasons.

concept (KAHN sept) *noun*   A **concept** is a general idea you have about something, based on information.
   EXAMPLE: *The **concept** of honor hadn't crossed Brianna's mind.*

devise (di VYZ) *verb*   To **devise** means to plan, invent, or create.
   EXAMPLE: *The scientist wanted to **devise** a machine that would allow people to float above the ground.*

distinguish (di STING wish) *verb*   To **distinguish** between two things means to tell the difference between them.
   EXAMPLE: *Babies must learn to **distinguish** between day and night.*

guess (ges) *verb*   When you **guess** something, you form an opinion of it without having all the information about it.
   EXAMPLE: *When I cannot figure out an answer on a test, I try to **guess**.*

method (ME thuhd) *noun*   A **method** is a way of doing something.
   EXAMPLE: *Isabel's **method** for grooming her dog required four different brushes.*

What is important to know?

City residents are surrounded by concrete and asphalt. Trees and grass can be hard to find. Yet these people often see wild birds flying overhead. Birds may be their main connection with nature. As you read the article, ask yourself: Should urban people help to protect wild birds?

City Life for Birds

You are walking down a city street, and there you see it: a dead bird on the sidewalk. It might be a common pigeon. It might be something more unusual, like a falcon or a hawk.

▲ **This wild Red-Tailed Hawk has survived in an unlikely environment.**

The **concept** of wild birds in cities might be new to you. When you think of wild birds, you probably think, "countryside." In reality, though, large numbers of birds spend time in cities.

As you might **guess,** cities can be dangerous places for wild birds. How can they be protected from the dangers of urban life? Is it even **conceivable** that wild birds get special protection?

WHY PROTECT WILD BIRDS? Sure, songbirds are pleasant to listen to. Seeing a flock of birds crossing the sky is a nice sight. More important, birds help humans. They spread the seeds of useful plants. This is especially important in urban areas, where plants may have difficulty growing. These birds also eat billions of insects. Many of the insects they eat carry disease, damage trees, and destroy crops.

MIGRATING BIRDS Some birds that migrate across North America cross over major cities. These birds face a specific kind of danger: buildings. By day, glass buildings reflect sky, trees, or both. Many birds get confused and crash right into the buildings. The lighted buildings at night, though, may cause the most damage. Some birds migrate after dark and fly low. They can be confused by—or even attracted to—artificial light coming from buildings. As many as 1 billion birds die this way in the United States every year.

Bird-lovers have encouraged cities to **devise methods** for reducing the slaughter. One way is to help birds **distinguish** glass from open space. **Methodically** pasted images of birds on windows act as a warning to real birds.

Another idea is lights-out programs. In Toronto, Canada, about one hundred buildings joined such a program in 1996. Lights in these buildings are turned off after midnight during periods of bird migration. A few years later, Chicago started a similar program. There, more than thirty major buildings now participate. In both cities, the number of dead and injured birds has been greatly reduced.

▲ Some peregrine falcons have become successful inhabitants of urban areas.

PERMANENT RESIDENTS You probably expect to see populations of pigeons in big cities. Believe it or not, some predator species have also made urban areas their home.

Probably the best-known of these species is the peregrine falcon. By 1970, this predator had almost become extinct. A small group of people refused to let that happen. The group raised babies born to captive birds. Then they released the young birds into urban areas. The birds' chances of reaching adulthood were actually greater than in the wild. With few enemies and plenty of rats and smaller birds to eat, the falcons could really thrive.

Because of such efforts, the peregrine falcon made a slow but steady comeback. By 1988, at least thirty breeding pairs were living in several U.S. cities. Instead of nesting in trees or rocky cliffs, they nested on bridges and on ledges of tall buildings.

Birds are part of the web of life. Maybe this is why many people want to protect wild birds, including those found in cities. Just how much time and money should cities spend protecting birds? For now, that is a decision each city has to make for itself.

WRAP IT UP

Find It on the Page

1. What factors in urban areas can be deadly for wild birds?

2. List three ways that humans benefit from birds.

3. Compare the situation of the peregrine falcon in the 1960s and in the late 1980s.

Use Clues

4. What do you think is the long-term future for wild birds in North America? Why?

5. What arguments could be used to convince cities to use lights-out programs?

6. What else could be done to protect wild bird populations in urban areas?

Connect to the Big Question

After reading the article, do you think urban people should help to protect wild birds? Why or why not?

Real-Life Connection

Most people experience a tragedy at some point in their lives. It might be the loss of a friend, family member, or pet. It might be the loss of a home destroyed by fire. What are some ways people respond to a tragedy? Think about whether their actions are positive or negative. Then take a moment to write your thoughts.

WORD BANK

report (ri POHRT) *noun*   A **report** is a statement of something that has happened.
EXAMPLE: *Each officer's **report** about the accident was slightly different.*

question (KWES chuhn) *noun*   A **question** is something that is asked.
EXAMPLE: *There was still a **question** about how to change the bike tire because the directions were not very clear.*

observe (uhb ZUHRV) *verb*   When you **observe** someone or something, you watch the person or thing carefully.
EXAMPLE: *To really understand Jay's coaching style, it is a good idea to **observe** him at a game.*

knowledge (NAH lij) *noun*   **Knowledge** is information that has been learned.
EXAMPLE: *It was Kitt's **knowledge** of healthy eating habits that helped her get the job as team nutritionist.*

form (fawrm) *verb*   You **form** something when you organize it or make it come together.
EXAMPLE: *A group of sixth-grade students is going to **form** a photography club.*

What is important to know?

Any way you look at it, tragedy is a part of life. People who survive a tragedy and people who are greatly affected by it can react in both positive and negative ways. As you read the article, ask yourself: **What can we learn from communities that have faced a tragedy?**

RESPONSE TO A TRAGEDY

Fog, rain, wind, and darkness are terrible conditions for landing an airplane. One autumn night in 1970, a pilot of a DC-9 passenger jet tried to land in such difficult conditions. A mile or so from the runway, the plane clipped tall trees and crashed into a hillside. None of the seventy passengers or five crew members survived this accident.

The crash—near the Huntington, West Virginia, airport—was a tragedy. Seventy-five people had died. **Knowledge** of the crash spread quickly. Americans across the country reacted with particular horror. Unlike passengers on most airline flights, these passengers had all **known** each other. They had all had something in common: the Thundering Herd football team of Marshall University, in Huntington. The passengers had been on their way home from a game. Eight coaches, thirty-seven players, and twenty-five fans had died in that fiery crash.

A DEVASTATED CITY There is no **question** about it: Any tragedy has a terrible outcome. When a tragedy takes away seventy people in a town of 60,000, the

▲ Rescue workers at the site of the 1970 Marshall University football team plane crash.

consequences are particularly horrible. When almost the entire football team of a small university dies, the students are especially hard-hit by the loss.

▲ **The Marshall University football team today**

The city of Huntington stood still. The mayor declared a time of mourning. He requested that all flags on city buildings be flown at half-mast. He asked individuals to show the same respect at their homes. A memorial service, attended by many thousands, was held the day after the crash. According to one **report**, the service was so quiet you could hear a pin drop. In the days that followed, funerals were common.

Marshall went into shock. Classes were canceled. Students left. When classes resumed, saddened students **observed** the empty desks of the dead players. One former student **reported,** "It was strange to come to class and not see those people you knew."

RISING ABOVE THE TRAGEDY Despite the shock and horror, the city of Marshall experienced something positive. Citizens pulled together as they never had before. Team member Nate Ruffin had not been on the DC-9 because of an injury. Years later, he described the feeling among citizens soon after the tragedy. "All the barriers were down," he said. "No race seemed to exist. No male or female seemed to exist. It was just all one heart, crying for what had happened." Former Huntington resident Ted Dingler remembers that "the community put its arms around the school."

The school began to move forward, too. The idea to **form** a new team soon came up. A handful of people thought it would be an impossible task. A much larger group believed it could be done. The National Collegiate Athletic Association granted Marshall permission to use freshmen on a varsity team. Nate Ruffin and nine other players of the original 1970 team were part of the new **formation.** A new coach, Jack Lengyel, began to rebuild the team, now called the Young Thundering Herd.

What happened on September 25, 1971, was glorious. On that night, the Young Thundering Herd united against the odds. Most of the players were inexperienced and still mourning. This **observation** did not seem to matter. In the last play of the game, the Herd defeated a superior team 15–13. The crowd of 13,000 went wild. The Huntington community had believed in the team. Coach Lengyel had believed in them. They had delivered.

In November 1972, Marshall University dedicated a flowerlike fountain on campus to the seventy-five plane crash victims. The words on the fountain plaque express the community's belief: "They shall live on in the hearts of their families and friends forever."

WRAP IT UP

Find It on the Page

1. Why did Americans react so strongly to this tragedy?

2. Why was the crash particularly horrible for the Huntington and Marshall communities?

3. State some of the negative and positive consequences of the tragedy.

Use Clues

4. Summarize Ted Dingler's remark about the tragedy in your own words.

5. Why was the win on September 25, 1971, so important to so many people?

6. In what way is a fountain in the shape of a flower a positive memorial?

Connect to the Big Question

Now that you have finished reading the article, what do you think we can learn from communities that have faced a tragedy?

Real-Life Connection

Can skills used to survive in the wilderness help kids cope with everyday life in the city? Fill in a chart like the one below, listing the article's title and subheads. Based on the information they give you, how do you think the article will answer this question? Write your prediction.

Heading	Prediction
Title: Wilderness Learning	
Subhead 1: Non-Classroom Skills	
Subhead 2: Practical Skills	
Subhead 3: Working for Better Laws	

arrange (uh RAYNJ) *verb*   To **arrange** objects means to put them in a suitable order.
EXAMPLE: *Celia had to carefully* ***arrange*** *the items in her backpack to make them fit.*

judge (juhj) *verb*   When you **judge,** you form an opinion or make a decision based on facts.
EXAMPLE: *Tomás was uncertain about his ability to* ***judge*** *distances by using the sun.*

knowledge (NAH lij) *noun*   **Knowledge** is information that has been learned.
EXAMPLE: *Shamila's* ***knowledge*** *of baseball history is impressive.*

limit (LI muht) *noun*   A **limit** is the point beyond which something does not exist or is no longer possible.
EXAMPLE: *The long-distance runner had reached the* ***limit*** *of his endurance.*

purpose (PUHR puhs) *noun*   A **purpose** is the reason that something exists or is done.
EXAMPLE: *A paramedic's main* ***purpose*** *is to help others.*

What is important to know?

Imagine that your best friend lives in a major city. She has just told you she is going to spend two weeks in the wilderness learning outdoor survival skills. Would you be shocked at her announcement? As you read the article, ask yourself: Should city kids learn wilderness survival skills?

Wilderness Learning

Sixteen-year-old Emilio is trying hard to leave his gang in the Maryland city where he lives. He has not been in the countryside since he was a little kid in Honduras. Today he is hiking along a stream in a forest. Tonight he will sleep in a tent.

Until two days ago, fourteen-year-old Tanya had never been outside the California city she calls home. Today she is carrying 20 pounds of camping gear in a backpack. She is struggling to climb a 10,000-foot mountain. How did these city kids end up in the wilderness?

NON-CLASSROOM SKILLS Emilio and Tanya are in two types of programs for urban kids. Emilio's is an outdoor education (OE) program. Tanya's is a wilderness survival (WS) program. No matter what these kinds of programs are called, though, they all have similar goals: to teach practical, or useful, skills and encourage the personal growth of the teenage participants.

What skills would it take to survive in an environment like this?

PRACTICAL SKILLS A practical skill is a skill that can be used in basic situations. What are some of the practical skills taught in these programs? The main focus is on how to pull together the basic needs for survival in the wilderness: shelter, food, and water. For a lot of urban kids, learning to do this is a totally new experience.

For them, there is something really exciting about learning to survive on their own in the wild. In WS and OE programs, kids usually bring along tents and sleeping bags. They carry easily prepared food and containers of water. They gain important **knowledge,** like how to build a fire for cooking and warmth. They pick up important skills, like learning to **arrange** branches and leaves to build a shelter, identifying plants that are safe to eat, and collecting and purifying water. They even learn how to **judge** direction by the sun's location or by looking at specific stars.

An outdoor challenge like this ropes course can be an opportunity to test personal skills.

PERSONAL GROWTH SKILLS Besides teaching practical skills, WS and OE programs have another important **purpose:** to encourage personal growth. Many of the kids who participate in these programs are struggling to learn some, or even all, of the following skills:

- trusting others
- overcoming fears
- working as a team member to solve problems

Even in familiar surroundings, it is not easy to gain these skills. Kids in WS and OE programs are expected to develop them in a completely unfamiliar environment. In the wilderness, they have just a few supplies and a handful of other people. Suddenly, they experience a huge shift in what they think is important. People begin to change how they base their **judgments.** Personal appearance becomes less important than how well a person works with others in a tough situation.

Gaining these skills may be hard work, but many participants describe their experience as positive. It allowed them to test their physical and emotional **limits.** A teen in the Big City Mountaineers program described facing her fear of heights. After hiking for days, she had come within yards of her goal: a mountaintop. Then she looked down, and she panicked. What did she do? "I took all the strength from inside of me and pushed until I was finished," she said.

The personal growth skills do not have to disappear when the program ends. The participants can continue to use them when they are back home. They may fear flunking out of school. They may not be sure how to behave when they see their old gangs. They **know,** however that they overcame fear before. They solved problems. **Acknowledging** the problems they face every day, and using their new skills to solve them, will help them succeed again.

WRAP IT UP

Find It on the Page

1. What kinds of outdoor skills do students in these programs gain?

2. How do participants' points of view shift during the program?

3. Name two personal growth skills listed in the article.

Use Clues

4. How might someone in a big city use some of the practical skills listed in the article?

5. How could you apply one of the personal growth skills in the article to your own life?

6. How would you evaluate the author's argument in favor of WS or OE programs for teens?

Connect to the Big Question

After reading the article, do you think city kids should learn wilderness survival skills?

Real-Life Connection

Read the following statements about sports. On your own paper, write whether you agree or disagree with each statement.

1. Women are not strong enough to be boxers.

2. Girls should be allowed to play tackle football.

3. Cheerleading is a female sport.

Check It Out

A stereotype is an idea used to describe an entire group of people, even if it is only true for some (or even none) of the people in the group. Stereotypes can have a little truth to them, or they can be totally false. They can be positive or negative. Whatever they are, stereotypes are always dangerous. They put people into categories whether the people belong there or not.

WORD BANK

concept (KAHN sept) *noun*   A **concept** is a general idea you have about something, based on information.
EXAMPLE: *The math drill gave me a better concept of fractions.*

examine (ig ZA muhn) *verb*   To **examine** something is to look closely at it to learn facts.
EXAMPLE: *Sabrina wanted to examine the new school rules about using cell phones.*

involve (in VAHLV) *verb*   To **involve** is to include or to have as a part of something.
EXAMPLE: *I know guitar lessons will involve lots of practice.*

narrow (NER oh) *adjective*   If you are **narrow** in thinking or choosing, you have a hard time being open to new ideas.
EXAMPLE: *Gabe's food choices are so narrow he eats only peanut butter and jelly sandwiches.*

study (STUH dee) *noun*   Scientists conduct a **study** when they test an idea or research a subject.
EXAMPLE: *Lia's study showed that basketball was the favorite sport in her class.*

What is important to know?

Imagine you are at a varsity football game. The player who scores a touchdown is female. The cheerleaders are male. Would this scene change what you think you know about sports? As you read the article, ask yourself: **Should some sports exclude males or females, or should all sports be open to all people?**

Fighting Sports Stereotypes

The boxing match is over. The crowd is on its feet, yelling and clapping. The referee holds up the hand of the winner as the champ punches the air with her gloved fist. She grins widely at her victory.

Yes, you read that right. It was "her" fist, and "her" victory. The winning boxer in this match was a woman, Laila Ali. You might find the idea of a woman boxer surprising. If so, you are not alone. Female boxers like Laila Ali have to fight for respect. Battling stereotypes can be the hardest struggle of all.

Women do not fit many people's **concept** of boxers or football players. People think that these sports are too rough to **involve** women. They think women are not strong enough to be good boxers or running backs or hockey goalies. Another **misconception** is that women hate to play rough contact sports. Views like these are based on **narrow** ideas about gender.

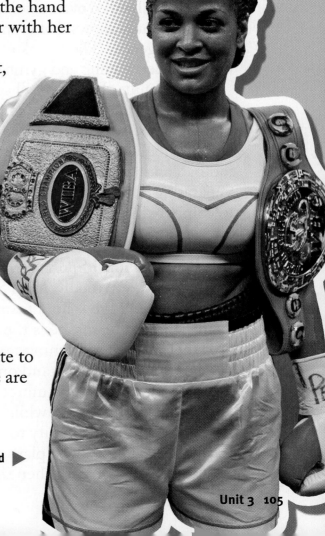

Thanks to women like Laila Ali, more and ▶
more females are in sports like boxing.

WHOSE SPORT IS IT?

Stereotypes about gender and sports are widespread. Laila Ali's father is Muhammad Ali, a world-champion boxer. He used to believe that women could not give or take punches. Then he saw his daughter fight. When boxing fans **examine** both fighters' matches, some of them argue that Laila is an even better fighter than her father was.

SHOULD GIRLS PLAY TACKLE FOOTBALL?	
Yes, in any league, on any team	59%
Yes, but teenage girls should play on girls' teams	8%
Yes, but all girls should play only on girls' teams	11%
No	14%
I don't know	6%

Information is from Heidi Coghlin, "Should Girls Play Football?"

Still, it is hard to overcome the idea that some sports are for males only. One **study** shows that even young kids have strong ideas about sports and gender. They think of football and hockey as male. They think of cheerleading and gymnastics as female.

Some adults think that all sports should be open to both girls and boys. Others think that girls and boys should not compete together. They argue that girls are physically different from boys and so should play sports separately from boys. Let girls play football and hockey, they say, but strictly in girls-only leagues. Separating girls from boys, they argue, gives both groups a chance to compete in their own way. Other adults think this is unfair. They claim that it keeps girls and women out of some sports.

NOT JUST FOR GIRLS Sports stereotypes do not affect girls alone. They affect boys, too. Kenyon Smith is a champion synchronized swimmer on a high school team. Smith is also on the U.S. national team. On both teams, he is the only boy.

Synchronized swimming teams move to music while swimming in a pool. They cannot stand on the bottom. They spend a lot of time underwater, up to a minute in one breath. Swimmers have to hold their partners up while treading water. It takes lots of strength and athletic ability to compete in this sport. Still, people tease Smith. They say he plays a "girls' sport." Smith just laughs. "I tell them all to try it. Then they stop bothering me," he says.

SIGNS OF CHANGE Athletes like Kenyon Smith and Laila Ali are helping to change **preconceived** ideas about gender and sports. One recent Internet poll looked at changes in attitudes about sports. (See the graph on the previous page for more results.) A close **examination** of the sports world reveals other signs of change.

In wrestling, for example, high school and college wrestlers are matched by weight. Girls can wrestle against boys in their weight class. Girls like Alix Lauer can win. Lauer prepares for a match by asking herself, "What's stopping me?" Her answer is, "Nothing."

Gender does not have to be the most important thing to know about an athlete. Laila Ali can be a strong, tough boxer one minute. She can be a graceful, gentle dancer on a television dance show the next minute. Being a boxer does not make Laila Ali less of a woman. Being a synchronized swimmer does not make Kenyon Smith less of a guy. Wrestling against boys does not make Alix Lauer a boy. The competition against sports and gender stereotypes goes on. The gender gap, however, may be narrowing.

WRAP IT UP

Find It on the Page

1. In what sport is Kenyon Smith involved?

2. List two reasons why some people think girls and women should not play certain sports.

3. How does Laila Ali break sports and gender stereotypes?

Use Clues

4. Where do you think young children get their ideas about sports and gender?

5. Besides stereotyping, why might some teams prevent males or females from participating?

6. Do you agree that people of either gender can play any sport, but they should play only with others of their own gender? Explain.

Connect to the Big Question

After reading the article, do you think all sports should be open to all people?

PROJECT: TV Commercial

Answer the Big Question: What is important to know?
You have read articles presenting ideas that may be new and important to you. Now, use what you learned to answer the Unit 3 Big Question (BQ).

STEP 1: Form a Group and Choose

Your first step is to pick Unit 3 articles that you like.

Get together. Find a small group to work with.

Read the list of articles. Discuss which articles listed on the left side of this page were the most interesting to you.

Choose two or more articles. Pick articles that you all agree on.

STEP 2: Reread and Answer the Unit Big Question

Your next step is to answer the Unit BQ with your group.

Reread the articles you chose. As you reread, think about what the Unit BQ means.

Answer questions. For each article, answer these questions:

- What is this article about?
- According to the article, what might be important to know?
- What do you think? Are the ideas in this article important to know? Why or why not?

Take notes. You will answer the Unit BQ in a TV commercial, "selling" your answer to viewers. Brainstorm ideas.

STEP 3: Discuss and Give Reasons

During this step, discuss reasons that will help your group sell your Unit BQ answer.

Discuss your answer to the Unit BQ. Answer these questions:

- What information in the articles is important to know?
- Why should people know this information?

Summarize your answers. Go over your notes and underline or circle ideas that you want to include in your commercial. Then write a short summary of that information.

STEP 4: Create Your Commercial

Now, make a final plan for your commercial.

Get a grabber. Think of the best way to grab your audience's attention. How will you make your ideas interesting?

Create a script. Be sure each group member has a part in the commercial. Write a script—the words each group member will say. Think about how you can convince your viewers about what is important to know. Use language that will persuade.

STEP 5: Check and Fix

Next, you and your group will check your commercial to make it even more convincing.

Use the rubric. Use the questions to evaluate your commercial script. It will be easier to evaluate if you read it aloud together.

Discuss your evaluations. If you answered no to any question, think of what you need to do to answer yes. If you need help from another group, listen to each other's commercial "practice" and answer the questions.

Improve your commercial. If your commercial could be more convincing or interesting, change the script so that audience members will "buy" your answer to the Unit BQ.

STEP 6: Practice and Present

Get ready to present your commercial.

Practice your commercial. Use your script to practice. You can write each person's part on a separate index card. Remember to use persuasive words and show enthusiasm.

Present your commercial. It is time to perform your commercial! If you have time and resources, think about shooting a video of your commercial to show the class. You can use music, special effects, and so on to help you sell your idea in a convincing presentation.

RUBRIC

Does the TV commercial . . .
- clearly answer the Unit BQ: What is important to know?
- include ideas from at least two Unit 3 articles?
- have a lively and interesting script that will grab audience members' attention?
- include persuasive language to "sell" your answer?

Do we need words to communicate well?

Most sports fans know two arms raised up mean "touchdown"! This unit explores communication. How important are words in getting messages across?

Think of at least three different ways that you can communicate that you are happy—without speaking. How do these ways of communicating show your feelings?

Real-Life Connection

A friend says a certain movie is the best ever. Another friend looks at you and rolls her eyes, so you know she disagrees. She told you something without saying anything. That is nonverbal communication, the clues we give without saying a word. Comedians use many nonverbal clues. Read the example below. Then explain what funny message is sent and how.

A comedian tells a joke about riding the train. She puts a hand up as if holding a train strap. Then she wrinkles her nose and looks at her armpit with alarm.

WORD BANK

expression (ik SPRE shuhn) *noun*   An **expression** is an outward showing of a feeling or thought.
EXAMPLE: *Ms. Lee had a joyful **expression** on her face when she saw our work on the poetry project.*

gesture (JES chuhr) *noun*   A **gesture** is an action or a movement of the body that expresses an idea or a feeling.
EXAMPLE: *Cara shrugged her shoulders, a **gesture** meaning she did not know why the accident happened.*

nonverbal (nahn VUHR buhl) *adjective*   Something that is **nonverbal** uses no words.
EXAMPLE: *Although Paulo said he did not care, his **nonverbal** expression said he preferred the pizza.*

reveal (ri VEEL) *verb*   To **reveal** means to make something known that was hidden.
EXAMPLE: *Jean was afraid her trembling voice would **reveal** how nervous she was feeling.*

Do we need words to communicate well?

You watch a comedy show. Two characters sit behind a news desk. One talks about current events. The other acts bored. He rolls up some paper and then uses it to play I Spy. You laugh because he is acting silly. As you read the article, ask yourself: How do people convey humor without using words?

Life Is a Funny Thing

Are you good at making funny faces? Making faces is a basic element of humor. Babies laugh at almost any face you make. It is harder to get adults to laugh, but many adults love seeing funny faces, too. There are even contests for the top funny face. One of the best is held in Egremont, England.

Once a year, Egremont holds the World Championship Gurning Competition. The word *gurning* is a Scottish term. It means "making a face." To win, a contestant has to make the craziest **expression** possible. Placing among the top contestants is harder than it looks. The winners are true comedians. They have figured out how to make people laugh.

LANGUAGE OF LAUGHS Facial **expressions reveal** thoughts and feelings. If a friend raises an eyebrow, it tells you something. He may not be sure what is happening, or he may be expressing doubt. Your friend may not realize his eyebrow is up. When gurning contestants raise an eyebrow, however, you can bet they have a purpose for doing it. They have studied how the audience reads **nonverbal** humor.

How do *you* gurn? ▼

You can learn a lot from these and other comedians. The face is not the only thing comedians put to work. The way they **gesture** with arms and hands sends messages, too. For example, a comedian might tell a story about being afraid of a bossy store clerk. The comedian's face **expresses** fear. Meanwhile, he holds both hands in front as a sign that he hopes to protect himself.

> When body language is used for laughs, it is known as physical comedy.

Comedians use standing and sitting positions, too. The way a person holds his or her posture can be **revealing.** A comedian might slump to show low feelings. You know what lowered shoulders mean when you see them. After all, if you slumped in class, the teacher might think you were bored.

Posture and other kinds of **nonverbal expression** are called body language. When people use body language to make others laugh, it is known as physical comedy. Comedians who throw all of themselves into joke telling tend to get laughs.

COMEDY CULTURES Physical comedy can be silly, like gurning, but it is not always simple. It can raise bigger issues. People from different countries live together in the United States. While that makes life interesting, it also means that not everyone sees **nonverbal expressions** the same way.

Facial **expressions,** such as smiles and frowns, are the same all over the world. Physical **gestures**, however, are not the same. For a comedian, learning what is funny and what is not is important. You might not think anything of it if someone sees the soles of your shoes. In some cultures, though, you must not show the soles of your shoes or feet. Showing them **reveals** the lowest and dirtiest part of you. That can be considered an insult.

A good comedian knows that not everything is funny to everybody. Some jokes may seem confusing or mean to some people. A comedian wants to let more people in on a joke, not fewer! To do that, the comedian reads the audience closely. The biggest laughs come from including everyone in the audience.

EVERYONE IS A COMEDIAN Successful physical comedians spend years studying what gets the most laughs. Physical comedy is an art form. One artist who practices it successfully is Jim Carrey. He has built his career on his ability to make wild faces and do physical comedy. When he was younger, he starred in a television movie called *Rubberface.* The movie tells the story of a young man who wants to be a comedian. He has to learn many things, including which facial **expressions** are most likely to make people laugh.

In many ways, we all study **nonverbal** communication to be more successful. People **express** many emotions **nonverbally.** We learn how to interpret the **gestures** and **expressions** of the people around us. When a friend is sad, she might need you to put an arm around her. On the other hand, she might just need to see a funny face, so you try your best at gurning. As a friend, you know what to do without anyone even saying a word.

WRAP IT UP

Find It on the Page

1. What is gurning?

2. What are three components of physical comedy?

3. How do facial expressions and gestures differ among cultures?

Use Clues

4. Why must a person who wants to become a comedian study what makes people laugh?

5. Are there any emotions a physical comedian cannot show? Why or why not?

6. Which would be more important in preparing to visit a foreign country—learning the language or studying the culture? Why?

Connect to the Big Question

After reading the article, think about nonverbal communication in comedy. Do you think knowing about this can help you in your own life? In what ways could that knowledge help you?

Real-Life Connection

What do you know about dancing? There are many different styles of dance. How many are you familiar with? Copy the following word web and write the different styles of dancing you know.

communicate (kuh MYOO nuh kayt) *verb*   When you **communicate,** you pass on information so that it is understood.
EXAMPLE: *Please **communicate** your plans for this weekend so I can make plans, too.*

language (LANG gwij) *noun*   **Language** is a system used to communicate, such as a set of words or signs.
EXAMPLE: *My grandparents' first **language** is Spanish, not English.*

nonverbal (nahn VUHR buhl) *adjective*   Something that is **nonverbal** uses no words.
EXAMPLE: *Red is often used as a **nonverbal** message to stop.*

symbolize (SYM buh lyz) *verb*   To **symbolize** means to use one thing to represent another thing, usually an idea.
EXAMPLE: *Our school uses the tiger to **symbolize** the power of our teams.*

Do we need words to communicate well?

Dance expresses thoughts and feelings. Dance also preserves and celebrates cultural heritage and identity. The newest forms of dance might seem like they are all for fun. As you read the article, ask yourself: **Is urban dance an important form of communication?**

Dancing in the Streets

You are hanging out with a bunch of friends. Music is playing. The sound of the bass rattles your bones. You feel your arms getting loose. Your feet start moving to the beat of the drums. Before you know it, you are heating up the dance floor. Who cares what your moves mean? This dance is how you feel right now.

Whether you know it or not, your dance moves have a history. Many modern U.S. dance styles have roots in African slave traditions. Slaves danced to help them forget their horrible living conditions. Drumming and dancing were ways for slaves to **communicate** and stay connected to their African cultures. They used dance as a **nonverbal** form of **communication.**

Dancers stomped their work boots to recreate the rhythmic patterns of drumming. This was called boot dancing. Some dancers slapped their chests and thighs to create different rhythmic sounds. This was known as hamboning.

The movements were a kind of **language.** Body positions **symbolized** certain things. For example, dancers might bend slightly at the waist to show their connection to the earth.

Break dancing is as individual as the dancers who perform it.

Most African dancing was done by individuals surrounded by others. Then, as now, this was a **symbol** of the importance of community.

CLASH OF CULTURES Over time, many cultures mixed with African slave cultures. In the late 1800s, "cutting contests" became popular. These were dance competitions, much like today's freestyle rap battles. Slaves and poor Irish workers took part. African tribal dance and Irish step dancing, or jigs, mixed together. Tap dancing came out of this mix. Tap was especially popular in the 1920s.

▲ **Successful stepping depends on teamwork.**

It is linked to the growth of jazz music in urban places, like Harlem in New York City. Dancers expressed themselves as individuals, but their moves celebrated their communities and history.

STEPPING OUT With the rise of new kinds of music, urban dance continued to change. A dance called stepping is associated with hip-hop music. Stepping is a line dance done in groups. It attracts people who enjoy teamwork and community.

This kind of dancing is not just fun and games. It requires background knowledge, skills, and rules. Stepping's foot stomping and hand clapping have roots in African dance traditions. Individual dancers use the rules and history to express themselves **nonverbally.**

Line dancers can compete as teams. The stronger the individual dancers, the stronger the team. College clubs hold stepping contests. These events are so popular that they are shown on national sports channels like ESPN. In large cities like Chicago, nightclubs and community groups host stepping contests. Such contests attract many young people, both dancers and spectators.

HIP-HOP TWIST In the 1980s, rap music became popular. It got national attention after starting in the cities. This new music seemed to call for new dance **languages.** One of them was break dancing. Break dancers twist, spin, and do windmills on the floor or pavement. The beat of a rap track does much of the **communicating.**

Break dancing is a very physical solo dance, yet it is often done in a circle of dancers. Krumping, a kind of dancing with free energetic moves, is similar. Krumpers do not break to the beat like break dancers, but they use their whole bodies to interpret music.

American tap dancer Savion Glover was influenced by break dancing and rap music. Glover combined street dancing, tap, and African dance traditions into what he called "free-form hard core" dance. He created a show called *Bring in 'da Noise, Bring in 'da Funk,* showing a connection between modern dance and African traditions.

Dancers in every generation create new ways to express themselves through movement. Even the newest moves, however, have echoes of old ones. People may not know the African traditions behind the dancing they do. The connection with tradition, however, is as strong as the best dancer on any dance floor.

WRAP IT UP

Find It on the Page

1. What is the earliest form of dance mentioned in the article?

2. What was boot dancing?

3. How was tap dancing created?

Use Clues

4. What are two common elements of African dance found in break dancing?

5. If you were judging a dance contest, what would be your criteria for excellent dancing?

6. How effective do you think dance is in showing emotions?

Connect to the Big Question

After reading the article, do you think urban dancing today expresses cultural identity, or is it just fun? Explain your response.

Real-Life Connection

Think about ads you see on TV. Some are good. Others are annoying. What else do you know about commercials? Copy the following statements. Next to each one, write whether you agree or disagree.

1. By law, everything in a television commercial is true.

2. Teenagers are a prime target for advertisers.

3. Commercials can make us want what we do not need.

Check It Out

Read on for some facts about advertising.

- The advertising business is built on communication. Advertisers communicate ideas about products to consumers.

- An advertising campaign is a plan made by advertisers. Its main goal is to make people want to buy a product or service.

- An advertising strategy is part of that plan. It is like a map or a set of steps that tells how the campaign will sell something to someone.

WORD BANK

correspond (kawr uh SPAHND) *verb*   When two things **correspond**, they match, are in harmony, or are alike in meaning or purpose.
EXAMPLE: *The team dinner will **correspond** with the final game.*

message (ME sij) *noun*   A **message** is a kind of communication that you give someone, either in writing or by a signal.
EXAMPLE: *Cara left a **message** on my phone to meet her at noon.*

share (sher) *verb*   When people **share** something, each person gets a part of it.
EXAMPLE: *Jay and Keosha will have to **share** the last cookie if they both want one.*

visual (VI zhuh wuhl) *adjective*   Something **visual** can be seen or understood through sight.
EXAMPLE: *Television is a mostly **visual** experience.*

Do we need words to communicate well?

You are paying close attention to a TV show. Meanwhile, advertisers are watching you just as closely. The commercials you see are not accidents. You are their target! The images are aimed at your age group. As you read the article, ask yourself: How do advertisers use pictures to reach people?

JUST ADD ADS

What is one experience most people in the United States **share** every day? Almost 90 percent of all Americans watch TV daily. The closest other **shared** experience, radio listening, is a distant runner-up.

With all those people watching TV, advertisers see an opportunity. Is it any wonder that they use television to sell products and services? If they have a **visual message,** they use TV to reach people. They also use billboards and magazine ads. Television, however, gives them the biggest audience.

Advertisers do not buy airtime on a guess. Much study goes into deciding when an ad will work best. Advertisers know who likes certain crime shows running after 10 P.M. They know who watches comedy shows. Advertisers place their ads carefully. They make sure that their products will **correspond** to the needs and wants of the people most likely to be viewing.

Think like an advertiser for a moment. A certain program is viewed mainly by young parents. Which product would have the best placement in this program—a sports car or baby food? Why do you think so?

Hours spent watching TV mean hours watching ads. ▶

THE CONSUMER GENERATION Teenagers are in an age group that has never been without television. People aged thirteen to nineteen have grown up with many brand names and commercial characters. Teens also have **visible** buying power. They spend billions of dollars of their own money. They also help direct the spending of billions more by their parents. These factors make the youth market a huge target for advertisers.

How much is the youth market worth to advertisers? You use one toothpaste at a time. You often pick out one kind of drink for your thirst. Dr. Marvin Goldberg studies advertising and youth. He says companies know that becoming your favorite can bring in lots of money over time. "Getting that space in your brain is what is worth an endless amount of money to the company."

THE POWER OF VISUAL CLUES Television is powered by **visual** clues. Things like books, CDs, and video covers are **visual,** too, but TV reaches the broadest audience of future buyers. TV images can bring out feelings in consumers. With pictures, it can send **messages** without actually saying them. When asked to name the most persuasive means of advertising, 66.5 percent of people said TV. TV scored higher than all the other major media put together, as the circle graph shows.

What kinds of images sell products? Usually, ones that make a product look good work best. Sometimes the **visuals** make you think that *you* would look good with the product! A cute girl drinks a certain soda, and the boys drool—for the soda, of course. If you look closely, you see that advertisers send not-so-secret

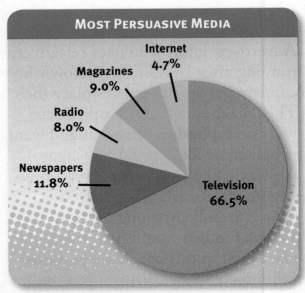

MOST PERSUASIVE MEDIA

Internet 4.7%
Magazines 9.0%
Radio 8.0%
Newspapers 11.8%
Television 66.5%

Information is from the Television Bureau of Advertising, "TV Basics: Image of Advertising in Major Media," *Media Comparisons Study 2006, Adults 18+, 2007.*

corresponding messages. They tell you, "You will be really cool if you wear the right jeans. If you buy the product that a celebrity uses, you will be happier." Such **messages** are not actually true, but they are powerful. If advertisers surround a product with happy, famous people, the product gets a positive image.

CONSUMER CHOICES Advertising performs a valuable service by telling people about products. Some advertisements, though, are misleading or stretch the truth. How can you resist those ads?

- Take a moment to rip the ad apart. What are the **visual messages** saying? Do any of them **correspond** to the truth?
- Ask yourself, "Do I really want this product?" Talk to people who have already tried the item. Do they think it is good?
- Can you afford the product? Will you have to borrow money or save for a long time to buy it? Is the product worth it?

Ask these questions to make wiser choices about what you buy.

WRAP IT UP

Find It on the Page

1. What percentage of all Americans watch TV every day?

2. List two ways teens influence the advertising industry.

3. Summarize two reasons today's teens can be called the consumer generation.

Use Clues

4. Why do advertisers use images to make suggestions instead of using only words?

5. Why can visual associations make it difficult to evaluate a product in an advertisement?

6. If you made a new law for the advertising industry, what would it be? Would it help consumers or advertisers?

Connect to the Big Question

After reading the article, explain how and why television advertisements communicate with images, not just with words.

Real-Life Connection

When was the last time you did something nice for a friend? You probably did it not too long ago. When did you last help a stranger? Think of some different ways to help people you do not know. Copy the word web. Fill in the blank bubbles with ways you could help a stranger.

Helping a Stranger

WORD BANK

connection (kuh NEK shuhn) *noun*   A **connection** is a link between two things, people, or ideas.
EXAMPLE: *My **connection** to the team is through Edgar, who plays shortstop.*

dialogue (DY uh lawg) *noun*   **Dialogue** is conversation between two or more people.
EXAMPLE: *The **dialogue** between the two actors in that movie was funny.*

reveal (ri VEEL) *verb*   To **reveal** means to make something known that was hidden.
EXAMPLE: *No one thought Kali would **reveal** her secret to Jorge.*

verbal (VUHR buhl) *adjective*   Something that is **verbal** uses words.
EXAMPLE: *She used to be quiet, but she turned into a really **verbal** teenager.*

Do we need words to communicate well?

Think of the last time you thought about doing a good deed. When was the last time you actually did a good deed? Talking is easy. Taking action is harder, because it takes more effort. As you read the article, ask yourself: Do our actions really speak louder than our words?

Acts of Kindness

As you walk out of a store, you are not paying attention. You are thinking about how late you are. Then you hear someone shout, "Excuse me!"

A woman is running toward you. She is waving at you frantically. She looks familiar.

"Yes?" you ask, wondering if you are in trouble.

"I am glad I caught you," she says, out of breath. "You left your wallet in the card store."

That is who she is—the woman who was looking at birthday cards next to you. "Wow!" you say. "Thanks so much. I did not even know it was gone."

What does this **dialogue reveal**? The woman could have turned the wallet in to the store, hoping you would return. She could have left it alone or even kept it, but she did not. Instead, she did something kind.

She performed a random act of kindness. Such an act involves helping people simply for the sake of being helpful. To earn the term *random*, the act must surprise people. The act can take many forms.

An act of kindness makes both the giver and receiver feel good.

It can be as simple as giving a **verbal** compliment. The most powerful acts involve time and effort. You might hand out cold water to people stuck in traffic on a hot day. Maybe there is a community center near you where homeless people find shelter. You might donate blankets there.

What do these acts **reveal** about you? More important is what the acts mean to the people on the receiving end. People will be touched by your kindness. You know what else? Kindness goes both ways.

Being kind feels good. That is why people who do random acts of kindness often get hooked on them. Knowing you have done something helpful can make you feel good about yourself. It can also help you feel a **connection** to the people in your community.

> Knowing you have done something helpful can make you feel good about yourself.

THE PAY IT FORWARD MOVEMENT Performing random acts of kindness has become a movement. A movement is born when people, even those unknown to one another, start favoring a common goal. It happens when an idea catches on. **Dialogues** about random acts of kindness take many forms. People have written books about it. Some organizations promote the idea. There is even a radio talk show that celebrates good deeds.

In 2000, the movie *Pay It Forward* brought the idea to a large audience. The movie focused on a twelve-year-old boy who believed he could change his world by "paying it forward." We often feel the need to pay back people who do something kind for us. When you pay the kindness forward, you spread it to others instead. You do something good for someone else as an investment in the future. Your deed may inspire that person to do good for others. This widening circle of kindness **reveals** how good people can be.

There is "a shift of attitude from 'what about me?' to 'what can I do for you?'," says a director of youth programs for the Art of Living Foundation. The group promotes the idea of paying it forward. This program involves teenagers in the Washington, D.C., public schools. Art of Living programs emphasize doing good things rather than talking about them. Directors relate that students tell them they feel proud to be friendly and kind.

A VERY OLD IDEA Random acts and paying it forward are new takes on an ancient idea called karma (KAHR muh). The word means "the force produced by a person's actions." Good karma is the good that comes from doing good things. Bad karma is the opposite. Kindness **connects** us to the world and the people around us. People who are kind feel more likely to experience kindness. There is no way to prove whether karma exists, but people who believe in karma believe that it works.

Sometimes a kindness is simply **verbalized.** Who does not like to hear that they are appreciated or loved? Actions, however, often speak louder than words. The next time you have something nice to say, stop and think. Is there something nice you can do?

WRAP IT UP

Find It on the Page

1. What is the biggest reason that people perform random acts of kindness?

2. What was the movie *Pay It Forward* about?

3. How did the attitudes of teenagers involved in Art of Living programs change?

Use Clues

4. What characteristic does karma share with paying it forward?

5. What random act of kindness could you do today?

6. Do you think one random act of kindness causes other random acts of kindness? Why?

Connect to the Big Question

After reading the article, do you think actions speak louder than words?

Real-Life Connection

Think of what you know about skateboarding. Then copy the following statements. Next to each one, write whether you think it is true or false.

1. More serious injuries come from basketball than from skateboarding.
2. One-third of all skateboard injuries happen to kids who have less than one week of skateboarding experience.
3. Skateboarding is good exercise for your heart and lungs.

Check It Out

Like any sport, skateboarding has its own language and key terms:

- **deck:** the plank of a skateboard that the rider stands on
- **trucks:** the metal pieces connecting the wheels to the deck
- **slide:** scraping the underside of the deck along a surface
- **grind:** scraping one or both trucks along a surface

WORD BANK

communicate (kuh MYOO nuh kayt) *verb*   When you **communicate,** you pass on information so that it is understood.
EXAMPLE: *A card can **communicate** birthday wishes.*

expression (ik SPRE shuhn) *noun*   An **expression** is an outward showing of a feeling or thought.
EXAMPLE: *She made her mom a cake as an **expression** of thanks.*

gesture (JES chuhr) *noun*   A **gesture** is an action or a movement of the body that expresses an idea or a feeling.
EXAMPLE: *Ms. Sherwin's friendly nod was a **gesture** of thanks.*

message (ME sij) *noun*   A **message** is information that you give someone in writing or by a signal.
EXAMPLE: *We got the **message** to be quiet when she turned off the music.*

THE BIG ?

Do we need words to communicate well?

Parks, plazas, and parking garages are examples of public spaces. You find these spaces in most towns. These places are great for taking walks and people-watching. Would skateboarding be welcome there, though? As you read the article, ask yourself: **Are public spaces really for everyone to use?**

DECKS & TRUCKS

If skateboarders see railings, they think about riding them. When they see a ramp, they wonder whether it is ever free to use. To skateboarders, these features can be like rides at an amusement park.

For many skaters, skateboarding is not simply a fun activity or a form of exercise. It is an **expression** of personal style. Skateboarding is a **gesture** that shows the freedom skaters feel as they play their sport.

Skateboarding has been around since the 1950s. In the past 15 years, however, it has become more popular than ever. In fact, the sport is one of the fastest growing in the United States. The country is estimated to have more than 13 million skateboarders.

As beginning skateboarders improve, the question becomes, Where is skating allowed? Skaters can only do so much on a driveway or a short sidewalk. They need open space and a variety of surfaces. That is why skateboarders go to public places, such as parks, plazas, and parking lots.

▲
Skateboarders use curved ramps to perform tricks.

Skaters are not always welcome everywhere. Many public officials **communicate** their dislike of the sport. Cities have laws about public property. In most cities, people are not supposed to ride bikes or skateboards on sidewalks. The people on foot could get hurt.

What about the open spaces of parks and plazas? Local governments want to avoid injuries to people there, too. They also want to avoid being held responsible for skaters' injuries. In addition, officials have expressed concern about the damage skateboarding can do. It can mark up benches, railings, and curbs.

THE COST OF SKATING IN THE WRONG PLACE

City	Fines (in $)
San Diego	50
Philadelphia	25
Los Angeles	100–150
New York	35–100
Chicago	35
Washington, D.C.	50

Information is from *Transworld Business*.

A PLACE OF THEIR OWN When a skateboarder grinds a stone bench, the trucks can mark the bench. Sliding can also cause damage. It can loosen or break handrails.

Most cities have laws about skateboarding in public places. Skaters can be fined if they are caught skating in downtown or business areas. (See the chart for fines in certain cities.) For a teenager, even small fines can add up.

Such laws do not mean that officials think there should be no skateboarding. Some leaders have made public **gestures** to skateboarders by building skate parks. These areas have ramps and rails made for the sport. Skaters can freely **express** themselves at skate parks. In 2004, there were more than 1,800 skate parks in the United States. Some of these special spaces look like big empty swimming pools. Others have ramps for special tricks.

Tony Hawk is one of skateboarding's biggest stars. He believes more cities should build skate parks. Hawk says when cities "build [skate] parks, they find more people use them than tennis courts."

Most skate parks do have rules to follow. Many parks require skateboarders to wear helmets and pads. The **message** is clear: You may skate, but skate safely. Other parks have a "skate at your own risk" policy. It is up to skaters to protect themselves.

PUBLIC SAFETY New skaters account for most major skateboard injuries. Experienced skaters know the right way to fall off their boards. Even experienced skateboarders get hurt, however. People who run the Tony Hawk Foundation and *Skateboarder* magazine understand the dangers involved. They work on **communicating** the importance of safety to skaters. Their messages are simple: Wear helmets and padding. (Hawk always wears protective gear when he skates.) When you start, you should practice falling in the grass. Never skate around nonskaters. Always obey the laws.

Even a sports doctor who has treated serious injuries sustained by skateboarders can understand why the sport is so appealing. He realizes that some people tire of organized sports like baseball and soccer. They like the free **expression** of skateboarding.

Skateboarding is one sport that athletes can practice on their own. Even so, skateboarders seem to find one another to share the fun. That is one reason that skateboarding will probably always be done in public. Skaters just have to investigate whether the public space they pick is open or closed to skating.

WRAP IT UP

Find It on the Page

1. How many skate parks were in the United States in 2004?

2. Which U.S. city has the highest fines for skateboarding in downtown areas?

3. Why do skaters use public places like parks or plazas?

Use Clues

4. What are some of the reasons people like skateboarding?

5. If you wanted a skate park in your town, what reasons would you give for building one?

6. Who do you think is responsible for a skateboarder's safety? The government? Parents? The skater? Explain your answer.

Connect to the Big Question

After reading the article, do you think public spaces should be for everyone to use?

Real-Life Connection

DO U TXT? *TXT,* or *text,* is short for "text messaging." It seems everyone is texting these days. It can be a great way to communicate quickly and without disturbing others. Copy the following statements. Next to each one, write whether you think it is true or false.

1. Texting began in the United States.

2. Texting while driving is against the law in all states.

3. The fastest-growing group of texters is adults.

correspond (kawr uh SPAHND) *verb*   When two things **correspond,** they match, are in harmony, or are alike in meaning or purpose.
EXAMPLE: *Leticia wanted to make sure her vote would* **correspond** *to the message she wanted to send.*

language (LANG gwij) *noun*   **Language** is a system used to communicate, such as a set of words or signs.
EXAMPLE: *They had been friends for so long that it was as if they had their own* **language.**

quote (kwoht) *verb*   To **quote** someone is to repeat his or her exact words.
EXAMPLE: *I* **quote** *the mayor's speech in my school newspaper story on community shelters.*

symbolize (SYM buh lyz) *verb*   To **symbolize** means to use one thing to represent another thing, usually an idea.
EXAMPLE: *A dove is often used to* **symbolize** *peace.*

Do we need words to communicate well?

Do you text? If so, how often? Many people text every day. Some do it to contact friends or to get work done. Not everyone thinks it is a great way to communicate, however. As you read the article, ask yourself: **How is texting affecting the way people communicate?**

Check for Messages

You are stuck in line at the counseling office. Your best friend is having a crisis on the other side of school. To **quote** her text message: "CALL ME ASAP!" She means, "Call me as soon as possible!" You think the problem might **correspond** to your upcoming birthday party. Thanks to your cell phone, you can find out fast. Your texting thumb starts flying. Problem identified: She only needs a ride.

Texting has come to **symbolize** the new ways technology connects people. Friends stay close, no matter how far away they are. Texting is one main way teens communicate. Teens did not invent the **language** of texting. They use it, however, more than any other age group in the world.

LONDON CALLING Texting has a short history. It started when the Short Messaging Service (SMS) was developed in Britain in the late 1980s. This service allowed people to send short messages between cell phones. The first text message was sent on December 3, 1992. The technology soon became available in the United States.

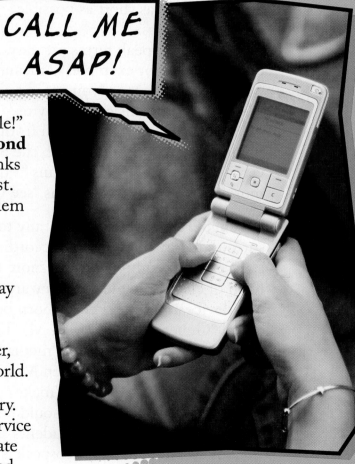

CALL ME ASAP!

▲ **When you text, your fingers do the talking.**

Unit 4   **133**

In 2001, there were 30 million U.S. text messages sent. In 2004, there were 25 *billion*.

Webspeak—the slang and abbreviations used in texting—cuts the time it takes to write messages. Cell phones have only a few keys. Each number key **corresponds** to as many as four letters or **symbols.** Making words as short as possible makes typing easier.

Some Webspeak terms are easy to figure out. For example, *U* means "you" and *UR* means "you are" or "your." Other terms are acronyms. An acronym is a word formed from the first letters of words in a phrase or clause. For example, the acronym *BTW* means "by the way." The acronym *IDK* means "I don't know." Other terms are more creative. *CUL8R* means "see you later."

Teens text more than any other age group.

IN TOUCH Texting comes naturally to teens, who have grown up surrounded by technology. According to a recent survey, people aged eight to eighteen spend more than six hours a day using some form of electronic media. They are often connected to more than one device at a time. People born between 1980 and 2000 are called "Generation M" (Gen M). The *M* is for "millennial," but it might just as well stand for "media."

Some people fear that Gen M spends too much time online. They fear over-use of media makes young people less social and less physically active than they should be. **Quotations** from educators say Webspeak is affecting students' ability to read and write well.

Not everyone thinks Webspeak is a bad thing, however. A communications professor at Georgetown University says, "The use of language in a new way is really a good thing. . . . Young people are at the forefront of language change." She adds, however, that "you need to use language that's appropriate to the context."

Texting and sending instant messages (IM-ing) certainly make it easy to keep in touch with friends. Teens can text while researching a school project or doing other activities. Texting allows shy kids to "talk" with people they might otherwise be too afraid to approach. It lets teens talk to friends in ways that cannot be overheard. What's more, Webspeak helps keep communication short and simple.

CATCHING ON While Gen M has grown up with these new forms of communication, webspeak has been like a new **language** for their parents to learn. Gen M uses these communication forms more than anyone. Still, moms and dads are catching on in record numbers. The fastest-growing group of texters is adults.

The two generations are starting to use the same language when they communicate with each other. Young people like communicating with parents by texting, because it is not in the usual tone. Parents like having another way to stay in touch with their kids. Some adults use Webspeak in the workplace as a quick way to keep things moving. Others feel this type of communication is too informal for the workplace. Many agree it is the way of the future. After all, Gen M will go to work one day, too, and these workers will probably use the language they know.

WRAP IT UP

Find It on the Page

1. Where was SMS developed?

2. What was the main reason Webspeak was created?

3. What does *CUL8R* mean?

Use Clues

4. Why, do you think, did Gen M take to texting so easily?

5. What are some of the benefits of texting?

6. How does a shared language like Webspeak serve young people?

Connect to the Big Question

After reading the article, how do you think texting is affecting the way people communicate?

Real-Life Connection

Pop art is art that uses everyday objects. Well-known products and people appear in pop art. The names of three pop artists are in the following chart. How much do you know about them? Copy the chart. Then fill it out by placing an *X* in the box that shows your level of knowledge.

Artist	Know a Lot	Know a Little	Know Nothing
Jasper Johns			
Roy Lichtenstein			
Andy Warhol			

WORD BANK

connection (kuh NEK shuhn) *noun*   A **connection** is a link between two things, people, or ideas.
EXAMPLE: *I feel a real **connection** to the people in my singing group.*

expression (ik SPRE shuhn) *noun*   An **expression** is an outward showing of a feeling or thought.
EXAMPLE: *A painter's work is a form of artistic **expression**.*

share (sher) *verb*   When people **share** something, each person gets a part of it.
EXAMPLE: *Please **share** your treat with everyone.*

visual (VI zhuh wuhl) *adjective*   Something **visual** can be seen or understood through sight.
EXAMPLE: *I need **visual** instructions to help me understand how to put all the pieces together.*

Do we need words to communicate well?

Wait! That empty soda can could be made into art. That gum wrapper could be art, too. Pop art lets you see everyday objects in a new way. As you read the article, ask yourself: **What does pop art tell us about our world?**

Everyday Art

Is a comic strip actually a work of art? Would you consider a painting of a spray-paint can art? Maybe you could paint a picture of a Lebron James jersey or a cell phone and call that "art." If you were a pop artist, those might actually be two great ideas for paintings!

Unlike traditional art, pop art uses everyday objects and images. Not everyone feels a **connection** to pop art. Some art fans think it is not really an **expression** of art at all. Other art fans like pop art. They say the real subject matter of pop art is popular culture. This kind of art allows artists to share interesting comments on their culture in a **visual** way.

▲ Why might this Roy Lichtenstein painting be considered pop art?

THE DAWN OF TELEVISION It is no surprise that the pop art movement began in the late 1950s. Television, which is very **visual,** was still exciting and new at that time. For the first time, people could sit in their homes and watch singers and other performers who were far away. They got nightly news from around the world. Unlike the radio news programs people were used to, television news could actually show viewers what was happening in other places.

TV stations needed money to keep their shows on the air. To get money, the stations sold commercial time. Companies that bought the time tried to make **visually** exciting products and advertisements. They tried to make images that would stand out in viewers' minds.

For the first time, it was possible for someone in California to see the same ads as someone in New York. TV became a way for people across the country to feel **connections.** The **shared** images became the basis of the pop art movement.

▲ This image was inspired by Andy Warhol's style of pop art.

WHAT IS POPULAR CAN BE ART Pop artists use popular images to **express** their thoughts about society. They put a personal twist on the images. Jasper Johns was an early pop artist. His 1955 painting *Flag* is a good example of pop art. It is an image of the U.S. flag. Look closely at the stripes, however, and you can see newspaper ads showing through the paint. Johns was making a comment on American culture. He was pointing out the large role that advertising was playing in American life.

Another pop art pioneer was Roy Lichtenstein. He loved the way color comic strips looked. During and after World War II, comic books became popular. By the 1950s and 1960s, color comics were common. They had become everyday art. Lichtenstein's paintings used colored dots and thick black lines like comic strips did. His paintings were eye-popping. Many were large, sometimes measuring 5 by 13 feet.

"Pop art looks out into the world," Lichtenstein said. "It doesn't look like a painting of something; it looks like the thing itself." He thought popular images affected people more than "museum" art did.

SOUP CANS AND CELEBRITIES Andy Warhol is probably the best-known pop artist. He studied art in college before moving to New York City. At first, he worked in the advertising business as an illustrator. This experience would affect how he saw and made art.

In the early 1960s, Warhol made a series of paintings featuring Campbell's soup cans. Campbell's was the best-selling soup in the United States. The can was an instantly recognizable image. It was not, however, an image anyone expected to see in art. Warhol's new brand of art attracted attention. He continued painting familiar products, including images of Marilyn Monroe and other famous movie stars. Warhol created album covers for popular bands. He worked on art for music, movies, TV, and literature.

Warhol became a very successful artist and businessman. His name and style were famous around the world. Warhol understood how closely **connected** advertising and art really were. His work influenced many artists and advertisers.

You can still see effects of the pop art movement today. Think of popular ads with colorful dancers and moving objects. The pop artists of yesterday, like Andy Warhol, helped inspire those ads.

WRAP IT UP

Find It on the Page

1. When did Jasper Johns make his famous *Flag* painting?

2. Who paid money to keep TV shows on the air?

3. What types of things are the subjects of pop art?

Use Clues

4. How did TV inspire pop art?

5. Where might you see the influence of pop art today?

6. Do you think pop art is as important as other kinds of art? Explain.

Connect to the Big Question

After reading the article, what do you think pop art tells us about our world?

Real-Life Connection

Background music has a lot to do with how audiences react to a film. Copy the following statements. Then note whether you agree or disagree with these choices for background music.

1. For a car chase, the music should be fast.
2. When characters kiss, the music should be loud.
3. In a battle, the music should be slow.

Check It Out

Here are some key terms about music in movies and on TV:

- score: music written specifically for a movie or show
- sound effects: sounds in a show besides music and speech
- soundtrack: all the music in a movie or show, often sold as an album

communicate (kuh MYOO nuh kayt) *verb*   When you **communicate,** you pass on information so that it is understood.
EXAMPLE: *I would rather **communicate** with someone in person than on the phone or over the Internet.*

dialogue (DY uh lawg) *noun*   **Dialogue** is conversation between two or more people.
EXAMPLE: *The **dialogue** between the two actors was confusing.*

nonverbal (nahn VUHR buhl) *adjective*   Something that is **nonverbal** uses no words.
EXAMPLE: *Our teacher raises his hand as a **nonverbal** signal for us to pay attention.*

visual (VI zhuh wuhl) *adjective*   Something **visual** can be seen or understood through sight.
EXAMPLE: *Painting is a **visual** form of art, but music is not.*

Do we need words to communicate well?

Have you ever noticed the music get really loud at the end of a movie battle scene? It makes you want to stand up and cheer. Good movie music adds emotion to the images you see. As you read the article, ask yourself: Why does movie music have such an impact on viewers?

Music Magic

The movie begins. It is night on the screen. The camera moves quickly, deep below ocean water. (You hear: *dum-DUM, dum-DUM, dum-DUM.*) You then see a woman and man run to the beach. She jumps in the moonlit water. She laughs as she splashes. (The music seems to sparkle.) The camera goes below water again. It focuses on the swimmer. You see her legs kicking in the moonlit water. Soon she screams, struggles, and is gone.

The opening scene from the movie *Jaws* is one of the most famous of all time. What makes the scene memorable has very little to do with **dialogue.** It has everything to do with how the scene was shot and the music that plays. People around the world know that the sound *dum-DUM* means something bad is going to happen. A movie's soundtrack is one of the tools filmmakers use to tap into our emotions.

EARS OVER EYES Music is **nonverbal.** It is meant to be heard. Other forms of art are **visual.** Hearing music is very different from seeing paintings.

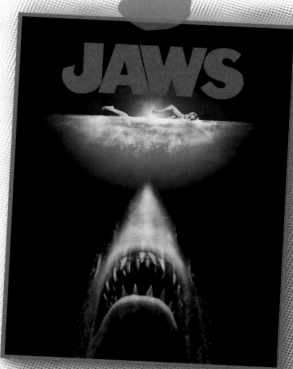

In *Jaws*, a young woman disappears below water. Music adds to the audience's suspense.

Unit 4   141

Music has its own special powers over audiences. It adds to any story being told onstage or onscreen. It draws viewers in.

Music has its own special powers over audiences.

William Shakespeare is perhaps the most famous playwright of all time. He wrote words to be heard, but he also understood the power of music. He used songs in many of his plays. The songs helped tell the story, but they also helped set the mood.

When motion pictures were invented at the turn of the twentieth century, they were silent. The technology to add sound did not exist yet. The first filmmakers knew music would help audiences feel the right emotions. They hired people to play movie scores on pianos or organs at the theater. Then "talkies" came along. The ability to **communicate** with recorded sounds changed everything.

SOUND REVOLUTION *The Jazz Singer,* starring Al Jolson, was one of the first popular talking pictures. It came out in 1927. The first spoken line in the movie is, "Wait a minute. Wait a minute. You ain't heard nothin' yet!" More and more filmmakers began including words, music, and other sounds in films. The technology of sound recording gave them freedom to use music the way they wanted. They could lower the volume of the music during **dialogue.** They could boost it when nothing was being said. They could use sounds in the background of scenes or as special effects.

In a scene where teenagers play baseball, you could hear birds chirping. You could hear the crack of the bat hitting the ball. You could hear a player breathing as he ran the bases. The filmmaker could crank up music that celebrated the game-winning hit. Filmmakers could suddenly say so much more **nonverbally.**

WHY MUSIC GETS TO US Why does music affect us so much? No one knows for sure. Many scientists think humans are somehow wired for music **communication.** We hear and understand music signals without even thinking about them. Some scientists think music may even have developed before language.

Music may affect the brain before the brain can even recognize what it is hearing. Scientists have learned that music affects the same part of the brain that reacts to a favorite food. Music is that powerful. We hear it and can have an instant reaction. It connects with our brains, but it also connects with our emotions. Do you have a song that reminds you of something special? Does hearing that song help you **visualize** certain memories? That is how movie music **communicates,** too.

Filmmakers connect pictures with sounds that bring out certain emotions. In a horror movie you might hear creepy music just before you see a monster. In a comedy, you might hear silly music when something really funny happens. The music might be slow and sorrowful when something sad happens onscreen. Even the toughest movie viewers might have tears running down their cheeks.

Film composer Michael Kamen once said that composers "are actors on the screen. You just don't see us." That may be true, but we certainly feel—and hear—their presence.

WRAP IT UP

Find It on the Page

1. When was the first talking picture made?

2. What makes music a unique form of art?

3. What are some of the theories about how music affects us?

Use Clues

4. How did talking pictures change the art of filmmaking?

5. If you were making a movie about what happened to you yesterday, what kind of music would you use? Explain your answer.

6. In your opinion, how important is music in a movie? Why?

Connect to the Big Question

After reading the article, explain why movie music makes such a big impact on viewers.

 **Graphic Organizer**

 Answer the Big Question: Do we need words to communicate well?

You have read articles about communication. Now, use what you learned to answer the Unit 4 Big Question (BQ).

UNIT 4 ARTICLES

Life is a Funny Thing, pp. 112–115

Dancing in the Streets, pp. 116–119

Just Add Ads, pp. 120–123

Acts of Kindness, pp. 124–127

Decks and Trucks, pp. 128–131

Check for Messages, pp. 132–135

Everyday Art, pp. 136–139

Music Magic, pp. 140–143

STEP 1: Partner Up and Choose

Your first step is to pick Unit 4 articles that you like.

Get together. Find a partner to work with.

Read the list of articles. Discuss which articles listed on the left side of this page were the most interesting to you.

Choose two or more articles. Pick articles that you both agree on. Write them on the Unit 4 BQ graphic organizer.

STEP 2: Reread and Answer the Unit Big Question

Your next step is to answer the Unit BQ with your partner.

Reread the articles you chose. As you reread, think about what the Unit BQ means.

Answer questions. For each article, answer these questions:

- What type of communication does this article describe?
- How does this kind of communication "work"?
- After reading these articles, do you think we need words to communicate well? Why or why not?

Take notes. Underline your answer on the Unit 4 BQ graphic organizer. Jot down your answer to the Unit BQ.

STEP 3: Discuss and Give Reasons

During this step, talk about your answer with your partner.

Discuss your answer to the Unit BQ. Give reasons based on things you read in the articles. Explain what specifically in the articles made you answer yes or no.

Add information to your graphic organizer. In the section called "How It Works," list main points about this form of communication. Choose details that tell why words are or are not necessary in this form of communication.

STEP 4: Find and Add Examples

Now, finish filling in your graphic organizer.

Get examples. Think about advantages and disadvantages of this form of communication. Use information from the article to add examples.

Write your examples on your graphic organizer. Underline examples that support your answer to the Unit BQ.

STEP 5: Check and Fix

Next, look over your graphic organizers to see whether they could be improved.

Use the rubric. Use the questions in the rubric on the right to evaluate your own work. Answer each question yes or no. Then trade organizers with your partner. Use the rubric to evaluate his or her work.

Discuss your evaluations. Explain to your partner why you answered a question yes or no. For every no answer, explain what your partner needs to do to get a yes answer.

Improve your graphic organizer. If your organizer is missing information or information could be improved, fix the mistakes.

STEP 6: Practice and Present

Get ready to present your graphic organizer to classmates.

Practice what you want to say. You will use your graphic organizer to explain your answer to the Unit BQ. Think about what you will need to say. Practice with your partner.

Present your graphic organizer. Explain your answer to the Unit 4 BQ to your classmates. You might discuss it with them, or you might do a multimedia presentation using an overhead projector, presentation software, or other methods.

RUBRIC

Does the graphic organizer . . .

- have an underlined answer to the Unit BQ?
- have the titles of at least two articles from Unit 4?
- include a clear explanation of each type of communication?
- give specific examples from articles to explain benefits or problems with this type of communication?

How do we decide who we are?

Can wearing a certain hat tell others who you are? Different hats change your look, but they may not reveal the real you. The articles in this unit explore the ways we decide who we are. You will read about risk takers and creative thinkers. How did these people decide who they are? How do you decide who you are?

Intelligence, creativity, talent, courage . . . how do these things go into making us who we are? Write a "recipe" to tell what makes you the person that you are.

Real-Life Connection

You may have heard some "rags-to-riches" stories. These stories are about people who overcame problems and became successful. Can people really become whoever they want to be in life? If so, what does it take? Test your ideas with the following chart. Copy the chart. Put an *X* in the space that describes how you feel about each statement.

Statement	Agree	Disagree	Not Sure
People have the power to change their lives.			
Some problems are impossible to overcome.			
People who are poor have no chance to improve their lives.			
Doing what you love will help you succeed in life.			

WORD BANK

conscious (KAHN shuhs) *adjective*   When you make a **conscious** effort, you do something on purpose.
EXAMPLE: *Eli made a **conscious** choice to get more exercise.*

expectations (ek spek TAY shuhns) *noun*   **Expectations** are hopes for the future.
EXAMPLE: *My dad has **expectations** that I will become a doctor.*

ideals (y DEELZ) *noun*   **Ideals** are beliefs or standards of behavior that people use to measure their actions.
EXAMPLE: *Honesty is one of the **ideals** I want all my friends to share.*

individuality (in duh vi juh WA luh tee) *noun*   Your **individuality** is the mix of qualities that makes you different from other people.
EXAMPLE: *Jessie shows her **individuality** by wearing unusual hats that she knits herself.*

presume (pri ZOOM) *verb*   To **presume** is to expect that something will be a certain way without proof.
EXAMPLE: *I **presume** we are going to have a quiz in science class on Friday.*

How do we decide who we are?

What makes you who you are? When you imagine your future, do you see limits or possibilities? Are we controlled by what others think and do, or are we in charge of our own destinies? As you read the article, ask yourself: How do we become who we are?

The Power to Move

Chris Gardner knows where he was when his life changed. He was sitting on the floor of a public bathroom in a subway station. At the time, Gardner was the homeless single father of a young son. Everything was against him. If you ask Gardner, though, he will tell you that this was the moment he started to become a success. In the subway station, he made a **conscious** choice to change.

Gardner never imagined he would end up on that bathroom floor. He had hard times growing up, but his mother had high **expectations** for him. She taught him to believe he could become anything he wanted to be. Life did not always match Gardner's **ideals,** however. His job did not pay much. His son's mother left them. He lost his home.

CHOOSING WHAT YOU LOVE

Gardner faced a lot of problems. You might **presume** that being a single parent was one of the toughest he faced. For his son's sake, Gardner decided not to stay stuck in that subway station. He looked inside himself and found the power to move forward.

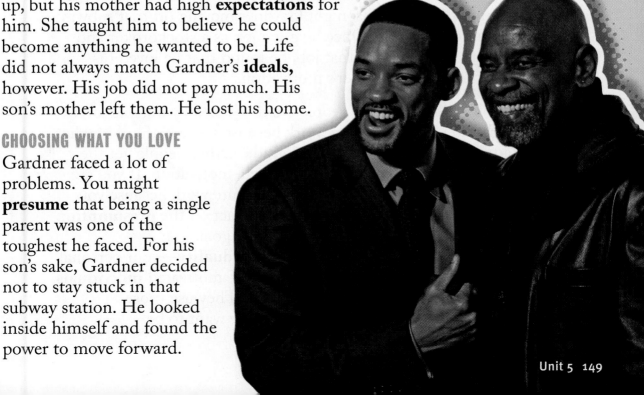

Actor Will Smith with Chris Gardner, the man he played in the 2006 movie *The Pursuit of Happyness.*

It worked. Today, Chris Gardner is a wealthy business owner. His story was told in a movie, *The Pursuit of Happyness*. When people ask Gardner for the secret to his success, he tells them, "The secret is there is no secret. It's the basics." He believes success is built one choice at a time. He tells people to work hard and to start with baby steps. "And more important than that, find something that you love," Gardner adds. "Something that gets you so excited you can't wait to get out of bed in the morning."

Use self-motivation to master a new skill.

To some people, Gardner's story has an **unexpected** ending. You may think his advice is too **idealistic**. Can people really overcome problems by acting **consciously**? Maybe Gardner just got lucky. Maybe his story is one in a million.

Chris Gardner would disagree. He believes his story can be anybody's story. The key is finding out what motivates you, or gets you moving. Love for his son got Gardner moving off that subway floor and into a new life. Once he got a job as a stockbroker and worked hard to succeed in that job, he found that he loved his work, too. Love was Gardner's motivation.

MOTIVATING YOURSELF Some people are motivated by outside forces. You might do your math homework because you are afraid of what your family will say if you get a bad grade. Other people get their motivation from within. That is called self-motivation. If you are self-motivated, you might do your math homework because you want to be a video game programmer. You act on the **presumption** that learning math will help you reach that goal.

Self-motivation is a mark of your **individuality**—your personal likes and dislikes, talents, and interests. Self-motivated **individuals** start with what makes them who they are. They use those strengths to help them to become who they want to be.

GET MOVING! Do you want to give self-motivation a try? Experts have some suggestions. You can use these steps to study harder, learn a new skill, or make plans for the future.

Do what you love. Find a connection between what you need to do and what you want to do.

Set reasonable goals. Do not take on so much that you get confused or so little that you get bored.

Break big tasks into smaller parts. This is what Chris Gardner means when he says to start with baby steps.

Stay positive. Do not put blocks in your own path. Thinking, "I can't do this" is an **unconscious** way of keeping yourself from trying.

Give yourself permission to fail. You will not always get everything right the first time. Do not give up, though. Learn from your mistakes.

Ask for help, and give it to others. Family members, friends, and teachers can help you stay motivated. When you succeed, encourage others the way Chris Gardner does.

WRAP IT UP

Find It on the Page

1. What job did Chris Gardner find that he loved?

2. Where was Chris Gardner when he made a conscious choice to change his life?

3. What is the difference between outside motivation and self-motivation?

Use Clues

4. Why is it important to do what you love?

5. How important do you think Gardner's positive attitude is?

6. Would the experts' suggestions for self-motivation work for you? Why or why not?

Connect to the Big Question

Did the article change the way you think about how people become who they want to be? If so, explain why and how it changed your thinking.

Real-Life Connection

How do you spend your time when you are not in school or sleeping? Some kids' time is filled with scheduled activities like sports, music lessons, or art classes. Most kids have some free time to watch TV, do hobbies, play games, or hang out with friends. Copy the following weekly schedule. Write each day of the week. Then list how many hours you spend in school (or doing homework), in scheduled activities, and in free time each day.

The Way I Spend My Time			
Day	School and Homework	Scheduled Activities	Free Time
Monday			

WORD BANK

argument (AHR gyuh muhnt) *noun*   An **argument** is a reason or set of reasons you give for being in favor of or against something.
EXAMPLE: *Tawana's **argument** against going to the concert is that the tickets cost too much.*

custom (KUHS tuhm) *noun*   A **custom** is the usual way to do something.
EXAMPLE: *For many, eating turkey on Thanksgiving is a **custom**.*

perspective (puhr SPEK tiv) *noun*   Your **perspective** is your point of view, or the way you see and understand something.
EXAMPLE: *His advice gave me a new **perspective** on studying.*

reaction (ree AK shuhn) *noun*   A **reaction** is something that happens in answer to something else.
EXAMPLE: *The crowd's **reaction** to the touchdown was a thunderous cheer.*

trend (trend) *noun*   A **trend** is a pattern of activity or a popular style.
EXAMPLE: *Gina keeps up with every new **trend** in fashion by reading all the latest magazines.*

How do we decide who we are?

Is there a connection between who you are and how you spend your time? Some people think kids should have every minute planned for them. Other people think kids need lots of free time. What about you? As you read the article, ask yourself: Do kids need to have all their time scheduled?

TAKING SIDES ON TIME

Two boys leave school on an ordinary afternoon. Sam races to his mom's car. He is lacing up his soccer shoes while juggling his backpack and violin case. Sam will have 15 minutes to get from soccer practice to his music lesson. Then he will grab a quick dinner before ending his night in the karate studio.

Sam's friend Jay takes his time walking home. He has no plans. Jay might listen to music, shoot some hoops, or play a video game. He might do nothing at all.

These two friends may not know it, but they are at the center of a debate. How should kids spend their time? Some people think kids today are overscheduled, or involved in too many planned activities. Others think kids' time is not organized enough.

Each side presents a strong **argument.** Both sides agree that the way kids spend their time makes a difference. What kids do with their time can affect who they are and who they may become.

TOO MANY ACTIVITIES Dr. Alvin Rosenfeld is a child psychologist who wrote a book about overscheduling. He worries about students who rush from school to sports, lessons, and clubs. "Kids today have very little time for a life of their own," Dr. Rosenfeld says.

Having lots of things to do can be fun—or stressful.

"And their lives are so programmed, if they don't have something to do, they feel bored."

What is the problem with a crowded calendar? Researchers like Dr. Rosenfeld list several reasons why, from their **perspective,** being too busy is a bad idea.

Lack of free play. Playing is not just for little children. People of all ages need unstructured time to daydream and be creative.

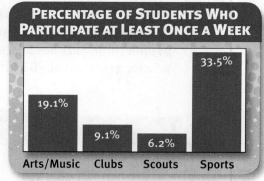

PERCENTAGE OF STUDENTS WHO PARTICIPATE AT LEAST ONCE A WEEK

Arts/Music 19.1% Clubs 9.1% Scouts 6.2% Sports 33.5%

Information is from U.S. Department of Education, National Center for Education Statistics, *The Condition of Education 2006* (Washington, D.C.: U.S. Government Printing Office, 2006), Table 13-1.

Stress. Some doctors see a **trend** toward stress-related illnesses in kids who are busy all the time. Overscheduling can lead to headaches, stomachaches, and trouble sleeping.

Pressure to be the best. Some researchers **argue** that many organized activities are built on competing against others. If a girl is not the best at an activity, she might feel like a failure. She won't have a chance to enjoy doing the activity just for fun.

Researchers also ask whether young people like Sam are overscheduled because they want to be or because their families have signed them up. Kids should not be forced into activities.

CHANGING SCHEDULES Dr. Rosenfeld's book came in **reaction** to changes in the way kids spend their time. Studies show that kids have gotten busier over the last 25 years. Between 1981 and 2002, in-school time grew by eight hours a week. Free time went down. Today, many young people are spending more time in organized activities. (See the graph on this page.)

TOO MUCH FREE TIME Some experts believe that it is **overreacting** to say that too many teens are over-programmed. They say the number of kids who spend more than 20 hours a week in organized activities is actually very small. Their studies show that young people like Sam choose to participate in lots of activities. They get enjoyment, not stress, out of staying busy.

This side argues that too many young people like Jay are drowning in free time, which can bring problems of its own.

Poor health. Those who are not involved in organized sports may not get enough exercise. They often have too little stimulation. They may gain weight from eating junk food out of boredom.

Not enough supervision. It used to be the **custom** for at least one adult to be at home after school. Today, most adult family members work full-time. Young people who are alone at home or out on the streets can get into trouble with drugs or gangs.

Lack of enrichment. Many schools today have stopped offering non-academic subjects like art and music. Researchers believe that the chance to participate in many different activities helps develop a person's talents and interests.

In the end, it is all about balance. There are only 24 hours in a day. What is the best way to juggle the time that you have?

WRAP IT UP

Find It on the Page

1. How many more hours a week did kids spend in school in 2002 than they did in 1981?

2. What is one reason that kids have less supervision today than they used to?

3. Summarize the debate over how kids spend their time.

Use Clues

4. Why might being overscheduled lead to stress for some kids?

5. Which side of the debate do you think presents the best argument? Give one reason to support your opinion.

6. How can kids balance organized activities and free time?

Connect to the Big Question

After reading this article, would you make any changes to the way you spend your time? Explain why or why not.

Real-Life Connection

You are getting ready to do something new. One part of you says, "No way!" Another part of you is excited and ready to go. Both these feelings may be right. Write one reason you would listen to each emotion.

Check It Out

Extreme sports, sometimes called action sports, involve lots of risk and physical skill.

- Skateboarding, snowboarding, and BMX biking are examples of extreme sports.
- The X Games is an extreme sports competition televised on ESPN.
- A halfpipe is a U-shaped ramp with steep sides. Skateboarders "drop into" a halfpipe by pushing off from the top edge of the ramp. Their speed helps them move down one wall and back up the other side.

WORD BANK

appearance (uh PIR uhns) *noun*   **Appearance** is the way someone or something looks or seems to be.
   EXAMPLE: *Auntie June's **appearance** is always very stylish.*

calculate (KAL kyuh layt) *verb*   When you **calculate,** you use math to find an answer, or you plan carefully.
   EXAMPLE: *I need to **calculate** how much money I made last week.*

logical (LAH ji kuhl) *adjective*   Something is **logical** when it makes sense, follows the rules, or is expected.
   EXAMPLE: *D. J. made the **logical** choice to study before the test.*

personality (puhr suh NA luh tee) *noun*   Someone's **personality** is the collection of emotions and behaviors that makes the person who he or she is.
   EXAMPLE: *Cheri's **personality** is bubbly and outgoing.*

respond (ri SPAHND) *verb*   When you **respond,** you answer a question or do something in return.
   EXAMPLE: *Lexi did not **respond** when I called her name.*

How do we decide who we are?

You love drumming. You decide to try out for the only open spot in the school jazz band. During your tryout, everything goes wrong! You worry that everyone will laugh. Whoever thought this was a good idea? As you read the article, ask yourself: Does taking a chance on the "impossible" pay off in the end?

EXTREME CHALLENGES

Pro skateboarder Andy Mac was thirteen when he first tried dropping into a halfpipe. Mac's dad was shooting a video of the attempt. His brother was cheering him on. Mac tried not to look down the 11-foot vertical wall. He swung himself forward, he went over the edge, and—splat!—he crashed.

Mac's father did not **respond** with panic. He calmly told his son to try again and kept the camera running. "I looked back up at the top of the ramp," Mac remembers. "Eleven feet is almost the height of a one-story building." However, he did not let the halfpipe's **appearance** stop him. "I climbed back up, took another deep breath, and dropped in," Mac says. "This time I made it! Everyone yelled for me."

What is it about Mac's **personality** that made him decide to skate down a steep wall the height of a building? It does not seem **logical** to try it the first time. It seems even crazier to get up after falling and try it again! However, Mac is not alone.

Skateboarders seem to do the impossible when they drop into a steep halfpipe.

EXTREMELY POPULAR Extreme sports have exploded in popularity. Sports like skateboarding and snowboarding feature lots of tricks and thrills. They can be risky and dangerous. People seem to love watching extreme athletes in action. The X Games competition draws millions of TV viewers. A pro skateboarder like Tony Hawk stars in a line of video games.

▲ This boy enjoys BMX biking on a bicycle track.

Young people do not just watch extreme sports. More and more, they participate, too. Experts **calculate** that involvement in skateboarding grew by 73 percent in the years 1998 through 2001.

DARING THE IMPOSSIBLE It can be hard to do something for the first time. Andy Mac's brain probably told him it was impossible to skate into an 11-foot drop. **Logically,** it is impossible to overcome gravity, too. However, skateboarders and snowboarders have been doing it for many years—ever since Alan Gelfand invented a move called the ollie. This move got its name from Gelfand's nickname, Ollie. It is the basis for amazing tricks. The ollie came to Gelfand by accident. He discovered it when he was about thirteen years old. He was skating part of a pool-shaped run that was vertical at the top. When he would hit that area before flying out of the run, it would pitch the board back to him. If he bent his knees when this happened, the board would "stick" to his feet while he was in the air. He found he could produce this effect on other surfaces by snapping the tail of the board down while sliding his front foot up the board and jumping. Nobody who saw this move could believe it. Did Gelfand have tape or glue on his shoes? Kids used to steal them to find out.

People once thought that climbing the Himalayas, the world's tallest mountains, was impossible, too. Edmund Hillary and Tenzing Norgay proved them wrong by reaching the top of Mount Everest in 1953. In fact, athlete Hannah Teter has snowboarded down one of the steep, icy Himalayas as if it were a giant halfpipe!

TO RISK OR NOT TO RISK What can you learn from extreme athletes? Even if you never drop into a halfpipe or climb the Himalayas, you will face many new experiences in your life. Every time you face a new challenge, you will need to decide whether to take the risk. Your **response** to a challenge can tell you about who you are. It can help you learn about your strengths and limits.

Some people claim that taking the right kinds of risks is a good thing. There are many reasons why. The most important is the chance to build confidence. Taking positive risks may help you feel more sure of yourself. Yes, there is always a chance that you will fall on your face. If you never try, though, you may never discover all that you can do. There is no magical **calculation** that will guarantee success. However, if you take a deep breath and "drop into" something new, you might just make the word *impossible* **disappear** from your vocabulary.

WRAP IT UP

Find It on the Page

1. How old was Alan Gelfand when he invented the ollie?

2. In what ways are kids who take positive risks different from those who do not?

3. Give an example of the growing popularity of extreme sports.

Use Clues

4. What might have happened if Andy Mac had quit after his first halfpipe attempt?

5. How could the media use the popularity of extreme sports to get kids to take more positive risks?

6. What conclusions can you draw from this article about what the word *impossible* means?

Connect to the Big Question

After reading this article, how do you feel about trying something you have always thought was impossible?

Real-Life Connection

Do you think you are a creative person? You might think of creativity as being good at art, music, or writing. Creativity can also be a way of thinking that helps bring new ideas and inventions into the world. What makes someone a creative thinker? Copy the following word web and use it to jot down your ideas about creative thinking.

Creative Thinking

WORD BANK

discover (dis KUH vuhr) *verb*   To **discover** something is to see it or understand it for the first time.
EXAMPLE: *You will **discover** something about how magnets work by doing the experiment.*

diverse (dy VUHRS) *adjective*   Things that are **diverse** are different from one another, or show variety.
EXAMPLE: *Students tried a **diverse** menu of foods at the international festival.*

reflect (ri FLEKT) *verb*   When you **reflect** on something, you give it serious thought.
EXAMPLE: ***Reflect** on the experience before writing about it in your journal.*

similar (SI muh luhr) *adjective*   Things that are **similar** are alike in some way.
EXAMPLE: *Ming and her twin are so **similar** in looks that I often mistake one for the other.*

unique (yoo NEEK) *adjective*   Something is described as **unique** when it is one of a kind or very unusual.
EXAMPLE: *The artist designed a **unique** logo that would help the new company stand out from the others.*

How do we decide who we are?

You are stuck on a deserted island with nothing but an empty bottle, an old CD, and a kite on a string. How would you attract attention to get rescued? Being able to think creatively might help save your life! As you read the article, ask yourself: **How does creative thinking help us all?**

The Creative Connection

*T*hink fast. How are a potato field and a television screen **similar**? How could standing in line for a fast-food burger help people understand American Sign Language?

These **diverse** examples have one thing in common: creative thinking. In each case, someone used creative thinking to make an unexpected connection. Then that creative connection led to an invention. Some of the world's most famous inventions came from the creative minds of teens.

Television is just one example. Yes, it is true. The thing some people call a big time waster for kids was made possible by a kid. A teenager helped find the solution scientists were looking for.

A NEW WAY OF LOOKING Philo Farnsworth was a fourteen-year-old Idaho farm boy, working his family's potato field, when he got the idea for a TV picture tube. Farnsworth had always loved science. He knew that scientists had experimented with "television," or long-distance viewing. People had tried scanning pictures and sending them through the air. Early scanners used a circular pattern to pick up an image. These scanners did not capture picture details very well, however.

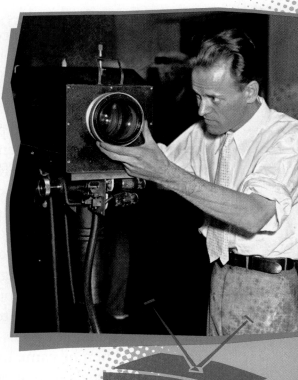

Philo Farnsworth used a television camera to demonstrate his invention.

As Farnsworth went back and forth tilling the field, he began to **reflect** on the scanning process. Maybe pictures could be scanned the same way: back and forth, line by line, just as people scan a page with their eyes when they read.

Farnsworth diagrammed his idea on a scrap of paper and gave it to his high-school science teacher. That was in 1922. Years later, Farnsworth went to court to claim credit for his idea, which led to the development of television. As evidence, Farnsworth's old science teacher showed the scribbled drawing he had saved. The court ruled in Farnsworth's favor.

▲ Creative thinkers are curious about everything.

A NEW WAY OF SPEAKING Ryan Patterson was also a teenager when he got a bright idea. He was in a fast-food restaurant and saw some customers who were deaf trying to place their orders. First they communicated to a speaking person by sign language, spelling out words with their fingers. Then the speaker would translate their signals for the counter clerk. Patterson thought there must be a way for people who are deaf or nonspeaking to communicate more easily.

He had been exploring electronics for a long time. In fact, he had already used his knowledge to invent a computer-controlled robot. What if he could make a connection between that knowledge and the finger signals he saw those customers use?

Patterson had to do a project for an upcoming science fair, so he put his creative mind to work. He invented a glove that transmitted the hand signals of American Sign Language to a computer. Then he came up with a computer program that changed the signals into letters and words on a screen.

Patterson was only seventeen, but his **unique** creative connection worked. This did not surprise anyone who knew him. Patterson had been experimenting ever since he could walk and talk. One year, he asked for an electrical extension cord for Christmas! People knew he would **discover** something important.

Patterson's invention earned him a $100,000 science prize. Better still, it gave people a new way of speaking to one another. "If I can make a . . . device that could help people out," he remembers thinking, "I'll feel as though I've made a difference."

A NEW WAY OF THINKING Creative thinking is not just for inventors and scientists. You can make creative connections, too.

Brainstorm. When you have a problem, come up with as many ideas as you can to solve it. No idea is a dumb idea.

Be curious. Ask lots of questions. Find out everything you can about a problem or task.

Open your mind. Do not stick with one way of looking at things. Explore the **diversity** of possibilities.

Make connections. Look for **similarities,** even in very different things. Remember the potato field and the TV!

Be willing to change. Inventors often make many changes to their discoveries. For example, Ryan Patterson later developed a smaller, more portable version of his translating glove.

The world may be waiting for a creative connection that is **uniquely** yours. You just never know, so be ready to think fast!

WRAP IT UP

Find It on the Page

1. What inspired Philo Farnsworth's invention?

2. Who helped Farnsworth claim credit for his idea? How?

3. Whom did Ryan Patterson help?

Use Clues

4. What motivated Ryan Patterson to create his invention?

5. List two qualities that creative thinkers have.

6. Can everyone use creative thinking, or is it only for gifted inventors? Explain your answer.

Connect to the Big Question

After reading this article, do you think it is important to be a creative thinker? Explain your answer.

PROJECT: Bulletin Board Display

Answer the Big Question: How do we decide who we are?

You have read about issues that make people disagree. Now, use what you learned to answer the Unit 5 Big Question (BQ).

STEP 1: Form a Group and Choose

Your first step is to pick Unit 5 articles that you like.

Get together. Find a small group to work with.

Read the list of articles. Discuss which articles listed on the left side of this page were the most interesting to you.

Choose two or more articles. Pick articles that you all agree on.

STEP 2: Reread and Answer the Unit Big Question

Your next step is to answer the Unit BQ in your group.

Reread the articles you chose. As you reread, think about what the Unit BQ means.

Answer questions. For each article you chose, answer these questions:

- Whom is this article about? What did the person or people in this article do that was interesting?
- What led the people in the article to do what they did?
- How would you describe these people to someone who had not read the article?

Take notes. On your paper, answer the Unit BQ on the basis of people you read about. How did they decide what was true?

STEP 3: Discuss and Give Reasons

Next, talk about your answer and start your bulletin board.

Discuss your answer to the Unit BQ. Think about how the people in the articles decided who they are. What images or words could you add to a visual display about the Unit BQ?

Start collecting bulletin board items. You might use article quotations and collect pictures from Web sites and print materials. Each group member might focus on one article.

STEP 4: Find and Add More Examples

Now, finish your bulletin board display.

Talk it out. Discuss with your group how you would answer the Unit BQ about yourself. How does each of you decide who you are?

Add examples. Add more examples to the bulletin board. Include examples that tell about each group member.

STEP 5: Check Over Your Work

Look over your bulletin board with your group to see if you can improve it.

Use the rubric. Use the questions in the rubric to evaluate your work. Answer each question yes or no.

Discuss your evaluations. Use the rubric answers as a guide to improve your work. You might rearrange items, add more color, add more specific ideas, and so on.

Finish the bulletin board. Use ideas from your evaluation discussion to finish your work. If time and resources allow, you might create a multimedia presentation to showcase images and sounds that relate to your answer to the Unit BQ.

STEP 6: Practice and Present

Get ready to present your bulletin board to classmates.

Practice what you want to say. You will use ideas reflected on your bulletin board to explain your answer to the Unit BQ. Think about what you will need to say. Assign each group member part of the presentation and practice together.

Present your bulletin board. Tell your answer to the Unit 5 BQ to your classmates. Explain clearly how the items on the bulletin board answer the question. If you chose to do a multimedia presentation, introduce your answer before showing your work to classmates. Be prepared to answer their questions.

> ### RUBRIC
>
> **Does the bulletin board . . .**
> - clearly show the answer to the Unit BQ?
> - have words or images that relate to ideas in the articles?
> - include words or images that relate to ideas in group members' lives?
> - reflect a presentation—color, layout, number of images chosen—that viewers will find interesting and easy to follow?

UNIT 6

How much do our communities shape us?

A parade and celebration bring people in this community together. In this unit, you will read about people in their communities. If you lived in a city known only for an unusual thing, how would it affect you? What if you lived in a community where adults mentored teens? Think about the Big Question as you read.

> Think about your own community. What is special or important in your community? How has living there affected you?

Real-Life Connection

Take a moment to look over the title and headings listed below for this article. Use the title and headings to help you write what you predict the article will be about.

Title and Headings	Prediction
Title: Help You, Help Me	
Heading 1: The "Helper's High"	
Heading 2: What Happens in Your Brain	

WORD BANK

community (kuh MYOO nuh tee) *noun*   A **community** is a group of people who live in the same place or share the same interests.
EXAMPLE: *The police officer worked in the same **community** in which she lived.*

family (FAM lee) *noun*   A **family** is a group whose members have something in common or are related.
EXAMPLE: *In my **family,** there are four girls and three boys.*

order (AWR duhr) *noun*   The **order** of something is how it is arranged.
EXAMPLE: *I always keep my music stored in alphabetical **order** so that I can find what I want quickly.*

survey (SUHR vay) *noun*   A **survey** is a way to gather information about a topic by asking questions.
EXAMPLE: *A **survey** of our class showed that the average age is twelve years old.*

values (VAL yooz) *noun*   Your **values** are the ideas you believe are important.
EXAMPLE: *Parents teach their kids **values,** like respecting others.*

How much do our communities shape us?

You step out of your local animal shelter after spending the day there. You walked dogs, played with cats, and cleaned a lot of cages. It was dirty work, and you are physically tired. As you leave, though, you realize how good you feel. As you read the article, ask yourself: **Why does helping make us feel good?**

Help You, Help Me

Oprah Winfrey's audience knows her **values:** She loves to help others and to give things away. Getting tickets to her yearly "Favorite Things" show is almost impossible. On this show, she displays her favorite items to buy. Then she gives all of them to each audience member. In 2006, she reversed the **order** of the giveaway. Instead of goodies to keep, each audience member got a $1,000 debit card. However, there was a catch. The audience members were asked to do something good for others with the money. They were now the givers. Winfrey said, "I can honestly say that every gift I've ever given has brought at least as much happiness to me as it has to the person I've given it to. That's the feeling I want to pass on to you."

How would you feel if you got $1,000, only to find out you had to give it away? Would you feel disappointed? More than 300 people in the audience did not seem to feel that way. They did amazing things with the money.

Oprah Winfrey hands out gifts at an orphanage in South Africa.

Unit 6 169

They started scholarships, saved a women's shelter, and provided training to disabled people. They did not care about keeping the cash. They were happy to help a person, a **family,** or a **community.** They felt great.

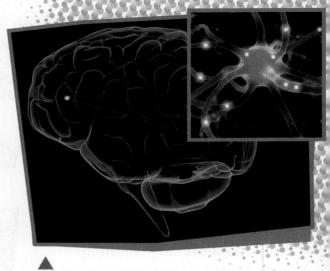

▲ The activity of neurons in a helper's brain increases during and after a good deed.

THE "HELPER'S HIGH" The positive feeling people have after helping others is called the "helper's high." Scientists have researched it for decades. One **survey** of more than 3,000 people asked about helping others. People who regularly helped others reported a decrease in stress and insomnia.

The helper's high can give you **familiar** feelings of warmth, energy, excitement, and joy. As these feelings fade, you then feel calm, relaxed, and good about yourself. These positive feelings reduce stress. Helping others can be very good for your health, just like eating right and exercising.

This helper's high can come from large or small acts. However, you might get a bigger helper's high if you want to help. Suppose that your parents take you to a soup kitchen at a local church. You are expected to serve meals, but you do not really want to be there. You are unhappy the entire time. With that attitude, you probably will not experience a helper's high when you are done.

WHAT HAPPENS IN YOUR BRAIN To understand why helping feels so good, scientists studied the brain. They started by telling people they would get $100. Then the scientists gave the people a choice: The people could have money taken from the $100 to go to a food bank, or they themselves could give money to the food bank. Then the scientists looked at what happened in the people's brains when the people made their choice.

For both ways of donating, the people's brains reacted. The area of the brain that reacts when a person is rewarded responded by sending out certain chemicals. These chemicals are what make us feel good. No matter how the people donated, they felt rewarded. However, for the people who decided to donate the money themselves, the reaction was more intense.

There are other **valuable** benefits to helping others. The same chemicals that make us feel good do other things, too. People who volunteer say they have less stress and pain than they used to. They also reported sleeping better. Helping others may lessen problems with blood pressure, ulcers, and cholesterol, too. The body's response to helping others is very strong. Even watching someone else helping others can help your body fight disease.

Think about ways that you can help in your **community.** Helping can be simple, like giving money to a worthy charity. If you can find time to volunteer, it will not even cost you money. Either way, pay attention to how helping makes you feel. Do not be surprised if you are feeling so good you want to help more!

WRAP IT UP

Find It on the Page

1. What is the helper's high?

2. List four ways helping others can improve your health.

3. Briefly summarize the brain study regarding helping others.

Use Clues

4. Why do you have to choose to help to get the helper's high?

5. How might people use this information to help people who suffer from stress?

6. Should schools require students to help? Explain.

Connect to the Big Question

After reading the article, what kind of community would you expect to be happiest? Why?

Real-Life Connection

Copy the chart below. For each subject, put an *X* in the box that reflects how much you know about disabilities.

Subject	Know a Lot	Know a Little	Know Nothing
Living with a disability			
Rights of people with disabilities			
Things that keep people with disabilities separate from the rest of a community			

Check It Out

The Americans with Disabilities Act (ADA) of 1990 protects the rights of people who have physical and mental disabilities. Among other things, the ADA requires communities and businesses to make public spaces accessible, or easy to enter and use, for people with disabilities.

WORD BANK

form (fawrm) *noun*   The **form** of something is its design or shape.
> **EXAMPLE:** *TJ's birthday cake was in the **form** of a football.*

group (groop) *noun*   A **group** is a collection of people or things treated as a single item.
> **EXAMPLE:** *Liliana belongs to a singing **group**.*

involve (in VAHLV) *verb*   To **involve** is to include or to have as a part of something.
> **EXAMPLE:** *The skate park committee hopes to **involve** more kids.*

isolate (Y suh layt) *verb*   To **isolate** is to separate out or to leave alone.
> **EXAMPLE:** *In science class, we had to **isolate** the salt from seawater.*

participation (pahr ti suh PAY shuhn) *noun*   **Participation** is taking part in something with others.
> **EXAMPLE:** *The class had 100 percent **participation** in the food drive.*

How much do our communities shape us?

What if everywhere you turned, you met a wall, a fence, or a deep puddle? For many people with disabilities, just getting around each day can be like running an obstacle course. This can make it hard to feel like part of a community. As you read the article, ask yourself: Why should communities make themselves accessible?

Making Everyone Welcome

What do you and your friends like doing in your community? Having a picnic in a park? Taking a bus to a movie or a baseball game? Going out for pizza, or just hanging out with your **group** at the mall?

You probably take your **participation** in these simple activities for granted. What if even simple activities were too hard? What if the park paths were too steep or rough for you to walk on? What if you could not climb onto a bus? What if you could not see which bus stop to get off at? What if the pizza place had no room for you at its tables? What if a door was too narrow for you to go through? What if the only bathrooms at the mall were on the second floor—and there were no elevators?

Before 1990, there were no "what ifs" about it for people with physical disabilities. There were many obstacles in the way of getting around. These barriers tended to **isolate** people with disabilities from the larger community. Life could be very lonely for them.

OPENING DOORS The Americans with Disabilities Act (ADA) helped open doors that had been closed to many people. It said that communities must take reasonable steps to **involve** people with disabilities.

This sign, a simple picture of a person using a wheelchair, has come to stand for a place that is open to people with any kind of disability.

Today, kids with disabilities can do many of the things their friends do. Park paths are smooth enough for wheelchairs. Curbs are cut so it is easy to cross streets. Most public buses now have wheelchair lifts. Stores and public buildings have automatic doors, with ramps leading to the doors. Restaurant tables have room for wheelchairs. You can see the accessibility symbol in parking lots and at the entrances to restrooms, elevators, and even amusement park rides.

These improvements did not happen overnight, however. Many communities still have a long way to go before they become fully accessible to everyone. In 2002, people with disabilities were asked to name barriers that kept them from **involvement** in social activities. Bad building design still ranked as the biggest obstacle. (See the chart for other obstacles.)

BARRIERS TO COMMUNITY INVOLVEMENT *Named by People with Disabilities*	
Barrier	Percentage Who Named This Barrier
Problems with building design (stairs, heavy or narrow doors, bathrooms)	43.1
Problems getting around in a crowd	36.2
Lack of transportation	31.7
Trouble with sidewalks, streets, and curbs	31.2

Information is from the National Center for Health Statistics, 2002.

THE COST OF CHANGE At first, some towns and businesses were not convinced that accessibility was a good idea. They put off making the required changes. The most common reason they gave was that the changes would cost too much. Sometimes it took force—in the **form** of a lawsuit—to get a company or a town to open its doors.

Studies show that accessibility is not as expensive as people once feared. "Just three stairs and an inaccessible bathroom kept me from enjoying the local recreation center with kids my age," one Maine teenager says. "But a few hundred dollars made the place accessible, and now I can play games when I want to."

In fact, many businesses and communities have learned that it is more expensive not to be accessible. If they are sued for not following the law, they may pay legal fees and fines. Those often cost far more than it would have cost to make the changes in the first place!

THE BENEFITS OF BEING OPEN Accessibility has real economic benefits that balance the costs. For example, people with disabilities spend more than $35 million a year in restaurants. The owner of a restaurant in Joliet, Illinois, was happy to add a ramp to his front door. "If I make my customers happy and comfortable," he said, "they're going to go out and tell a friend. That's the best advertising you can get."

However, ending **isolation** for people with disabilities has benefits that go far beyond money. Accessibility helps these people feel better about themselves than they would otherwise. They can get more **involved** in the larger community. "Because of the ADA, I have more of the opportunities other people have," says one Kansas resident. "Now I feel like a **participant** in life, not a spectator." When communities welcome everyone, everyone gains.

WRAP IT UP

Find It on the Page

1. What law helped open doors for people with disabilities?

2. In 2002, what did people with disabilities list as the biggest obstacle to community participation?

3. List two changes communities can make to be more accessible.

Use Clues

4. What could your school do to make itself more welcoming to people with disabilities?

5. Other than cost, why might some places hesitate to become more accessible?

6. What are two ways making communities accessible could help people who do not have disabilities? Explain.

Connect to the Big Question

After reading the article, what would you say to someone who argued that making communities accessible is costly and unnecessary?

Real-Life Connection

Who helps young people succeed in life? Copy the graphic organizer below on your own paper. Then jot down your ideas about each group and the ways each helps kids succeed.

Group	Effect on Kids' Success
Parents and family	
Teachers	
Community	

WORD BANK

generation (je nuh RAY shuhn) *noun*   A **generation** is a group of people who are about the same age.
EXAMPLE: *Not many people in our grandparents' generation know how to send text messages.*

influence (IN floo uhns) *noun*   An **influence** is the effect that someone or something has on you.
EXAMPLE: *Rikki's track coach had a good influence on her running style.*

involve (in VAHLV) *verb*   To **involve** is to include or to have as a part of something.
EXAMPLE: *I do not want to involve you in my argument with her.*

judge (juhj) *verb*   When you **judge**, you form an opinion or make a decision based on facts.
EXAMPLE: *How did you judge the candidates for student council?*

support (suh PAWRT) *verb*   To **support** something is to show that it is true, to be in favor of it, or to help it succeed.
EXAMPLE: *Phan said he would support the school's new cell phone policy.*

How much do our communities shape us?

A recent TV "reality" show featured a group of kids left alone in the desert. They had no adult rules—and no adult help, either. That situation might seem like a great idea. However, can kids really succeed without caring adults in their lives? As you read the article, ask yourself: **How can adults help kids succeed?**

Mentors Make a Difference

Where would Luke Skywalker be without Obi-Wan Kenobi? Would Frodo have become a hero without the **influence** of Gandalf? Great adventure heroes have one thing in common. They do not succeed alone. Whether in an on-screen fantasy or in real life, young people often need help.

You may have lots of talent and energy. Your friends may **support** you. Still, at some point, you are probably going to need the wisdom of someone from an older **generation.** Someone who has been where you are might be able to guide and inspire you—or give you the push you need.

CLOSE TO HOME Adults who guide young people toward success are known as mentors. The original Mentor was a character in one of the world's first adventure stories, the ancient Greek epic the *Odyssey.* Mentor was the teacher of the hero's son.

Many kids find mentors close to home. A survey asked teens whom they see as role models. Teens **judged** parents to be their most important mentors.

▲ Community members who serve as mentors can help kids succeed in school.

Family mentors were far more **influential** than sports stars and musicians. "It's apparent that while kids look up to many people in our society, it's those who are **involved** in their daily lives who have the most impact," the survey director said.

Champion golfer Tiger Woods is proud to have had his dad as a mentor. "My dad was my best friend and greatest role model," Tiger says. "I wouldn't be where I am today without him."

TEACHERS AS MENTORS Teachers were in the survey, too. Like the original Mentor, teachers guide and challenge young people. Popular movies like *Take the Lead* and *Freedom Writers* were based on the true stories of remarkable teachers. These mentors taught kids about life while teaching dance and creative writing.

Would you willingly come to school two hours ahead of time and stay two hours late? Kids in Rafe Esquith's Los Angeles class do that every day. In their **judgment,** it is worth it. For more than twenty years, Esquith has worked overtime to mentor his students. Both teacher's and students' hard work pays off. Most of the students are from families who are struggling. Still, many of the students score in the top 5 to 10 percent of the country and have gone on to good colleges and careers.

THE LARGER COMMUNITY

An old African proverb says, "It takes a village to raise a child." That means the whole community can have a **supportive** role in a young person's success.

HELPING YOUNG PEOPLE *THE GAP BETWEEN WHAT ADULTS SAY AND WHAT THEY DO*		
Action	Adults Who Say It Is Important	Adults Who Actually Do It
Help kids make good decisions	76%	41%
Have meaningful conversations with kids	75%	34%
Recognize positive behavior by kids	65%	22%
Look out for the well-being of kids in the neighborhood	63%	35%

Information is from the SEARCH Institute, 2001.

Adults can volunteer to be mentors, working one-on-one with young people. In 2005, about 3 million American adults did just that. They spent time with kids, sharing interests and cheering the kids' successes.

Whole communities can also be mentors. They can sponsor programs to help young people succeed in life. In Boston, for example, teens from the city get a chance to learn about organic farming. They work with adult farmers in community gardens. They help other people, too. The food they grow goes to food banks and soup kitchens.

HELP WANTED Most people agree that contact with caring adults can make a difference to kids. There is a gap, however, between what many adults say is important and what they actually do. Most adults believe it is important to help kids focus on their education. A lot of adults volunteer as tutors. This level of **involvement** may not be matched in other areas, though. According to one study, adults are not doing what they say should be done. (See the table on the previous page for more information.)

Paging all those Obi-Wans out there! For many adults, it is time to follow their own advice. Young people could use their help to become heroes in the adventure story of life.

WRAP IT UP

Find It on the Page

1. Who was golfer Tiger Woods's mentor and role model?

2. How many American adults volunteered to mentor in 2005?

3. Why do Rafe Esquith's students think it is worth coming to school early and staying late?

Use Clues

4. Why might teens look up to parents and teachers more than they do to famous people?

5. Do you agree that "it takes a village to raise a child"? Explain.

6. Give two examples of how individuals or communities can recognize positive behavior by kids.

Connect to the Big Question

After reading this article, how important would you say it is for adults in your community to support young people?

Real-Life Connection

Read the three statements below. On your own paper, write whether you agree or disagree with each statement.

1. Communities, like individual people, have reputations.
2. A community can change what people think of it.
3. What happened in my community in the past has no effect on me today.

Check It Out

A mysterious crash happened in a rancher's field outside Roswell, New Mexico, in 1947. At first, officials said the wreckage came from "a flying disc," an alien spacecraft. The story quickly changed, though. The U.S. Army claimed that a weather balloon had crashed. Many people think that a UFO—an unidentified flying object from space—did crash near Roswell. They wonder whether the truth has been hidden.

WORD BANK

belief (buh LEEF) *noun*   A **belief** is an idea that one feels is true or important.
EXAMPLE: *Belief in freedom draws many immigrants to America.*

body (BAH dee) *noun*   The **body** is the physical form or main portion of something.
EXAMPLE: *The body of the novel takes place on a small farm.*

common (KAH muhn) *adjective*   Something that is **common** is ordinary or shared by a number of people.
EXAMPLE: *The middle school and the high school share a common athletic field.*

history (HIS tuh ree) *noun*   **History** is an account of things that happened in the past.
EXAMPLE: *Jenna found a Web site with a history of snowboarding.*

pattern (PA tuhrn) *noun*   A **pattern** is a repeated series of events or details that you can identify.
EXAMPLE: *Hiro has a pattern of renting a movie every Friday.*

How much do our communities shape us?

Suppose you heard a friend was from Hollywood. Would you automatically think she was a movie star? If a classmate moved to your town from New Orleans, would you assume he was a victim of Hurricane Katrina? As you read the article, ask yourself: **How does a community's past affect people in the present?**

LIVING WITH THE PAST

How would you like to be known as "the kid from the groundhog town"? What if everyone seemed to think Martians were your neighbors? For kids in Punxsutawney, Pennsylvania, or Roswell, New Mexico, those are not just silly questions.

It is hard to go anywhere in Punxsutawney without running into a groundhog. Pictures of the animal's chunky **body** are everywhere. The high-school teams are even named the Chucks. *Woodchuck* is another **common** name for groundhogs.

Punxsutawney is a small town. Only a few thousand people live there. Every February 2, however, all that changes. Thousands of tourists come to town. Millions more people watch on live TV. They all are focused on a very important rodent: Punxsutawney Phil. Visitors and viewers share one **belief.** They think the town's pet groundhog can predict the weather.

FROM SAND FLIES TO GROUNDHOGS Punxsy, as locals call Punxsutawney, did not start out as a groundhog town. In the Delaware Indian language, the town's name means "the town of the sand flies." **Nobody** seemed to pay attention to the groundhogs there until German farmers began to settle the area.

▲ If you live in Punxsutawney, you cannot avoid the groundhog.

The farmers brought a bit of folklore from their homeland. In Germany, people **believed** that February 2 was an important weather day. A cloudy day meant spring would come soon. A sunny day meant winter would last a long time yet. The farmers used the groundhog as a weather test. They watched what happened when a groundhog came out of its den on February 2. If the groundhog saw its own shadow, the day was too sunny. The farmers got ready for six more weeks of snow and ice.

People in Punxsutawney were proud of their groundhog. They claimed it was the best at predicting weather. More than a hundred years ago, they began welcoming tourists. They invited everyone to come see what Phil did on February 2. The rest is **history.** A 1993 movie called *Groundhog Day* made the town even more popular— at least for one day a year.

In Roswell, New Mexico, even parking garages welcome space aliens.

A PLACE WITH A STORY What is it like to grow up in Punxsy? One resident's mom ran a Groundhog Day souvenir stand when he was a teen. "From stuffed groundhogs to cookie cutters, face masks to seat cushions, books to key chains, it was all organized at our place," he remembers.

When he went away to college and to travel, people thought he was joking about his hometown: "People thought Punxsutawney had been invented by Hollywood screenwriters." The young man eventually settled in Pittsburgh, Pennsylvania. At first, he was happy to move away. Then he began to miss the town's friendliness. He liked being part of a place with a story.

"ALIENS WELCOME" Kids in Roswell, New Mexico, live with an **uncommon** community story of their own. For years after the mysterious 1947 crash in the rancher's field, Roswell remained a quiet town. In 1979, that situation began to change. People started to claim that a UFO really *had* crashed. There were even rumors of alien **bodies**—"little green men"—found in the wreckage. Sci-fi fans and UFO **believers** started visiting Roswell.

Roswell followed the **pattern** of towns like Punxsy. The community now earns tourist money from its **history.** Today, the town has a UFO Museum that draws more than 150,000 visitors each year. The city's street lamps are designed to **embody** glowing alien faces. Signs throughout the town read "Aliens Welcome!"

NOT ALL HAPPY ENDINGS It is not always easy to live in a **historical** community. Some Punxsy residents may be tired of hearing about February 2. Many people in Roswell may find aliens boring. Just imagine if people knew your community only as the site of a terrible disaster. You would probably hate the media's being there so often.

A community's past can affect life in the present. Communities are shaped by the stories they tell and the way they tell them.

WRAP IT UP

Find It on the Page

1. What does the name Punxsutawney mean?

2. According to the article, what does it mean if a groundhog sees his shadow on February 2?

3. What incident made Roswell, New Mexico, famous?

Use Clues

4. Why might some people have a hard time believing that Punxsutawney is a real place?

5. What do the two communities in this article have in common?

6. Would you like to live in a small community that draws thousands of tourists? Why or why not?

Connect to the Big Question

After reading this article, how do you think a community's past can affect its people in the present? Explain.

Real-Life Connection

Preview the article title and headings below. On your own paper, jot down what you think this article will be discussing.

Title and Headings	Prediction
Title: Seeking Student Success	
Heading 1: Rewards as Motivation	
Heading 2: Drawbacks of Rewards	
Heading 3: Pride as Motivation	

WORD BANK

belief (buh LEEF) *noun*   A **belief** is an idea that one feels is true or important.
  EXAMPLE: *Tino's **belief** in hard work helped him get ahead.*

connection (kuh NEK shuhn) *noun*   A **connection** is a link between two things, people, or ideas.
  EXAMPLE: *I lost my Internet **connection** right in the middle of my homework.*

participation (pahr ti suh PAY shuhn) *noun*   **Participation** is taking part in something with others.
  EXAMPLE: *The principal thanked the students for their **participation** in the car wash.*

prepare (pri PER) *verb*   To **prepare** is to plan or get ready for something.
  EXAMPLE: *I always **prepare** for a run by warming up and stretching.*

support (suh PAWRT) *verb*   To **support** something is to show that it is true, to be in favor of it, or to help it succeed.
  EXAMPLE: *Rowan said she would **support** Tim for president of the French club.*

How much do our communities shape us?

Which would make you work harder in school—the pride of bringing home good grades, or the chance to win a new MP3 player? It is a choice some students around the country are facing. Think the answer is easy? Maybe there is more to it. As you read the article, ask yourself: Should communities pay students to succeed?

Seeking Student Success

Jacob took four advanced placement tests last year. He had to study hard to **prepare,** but if he did well, he would get a bonus. He wound up getting $50 for each passing score. Dani just got a new cell phone as a reward for not missing a day of school. Luisa was offered $500 in college money if she graduated from high school.

Are you envious? You might think these teens have generous families. Many parents **support** their kids' efforts to succeed in school by giving rewards. However, the rewards for Jacob, Dani, Luisa, and other kids did not come from families. They came from the larger community.

Why would communities pay kids to succeed in school? Is paying a good idea?

REWARDS AS MOTIVATION The **belief** that students work better for prizes than they would otherwise is growing. Leaders hope that rewards will encourage kids to stay in school. They argue that kids will work harder if a prize is in sight. Teens who might otherwise be too bored in class will increase their **participation.** Students from poor families will be able to afford college. Kids will feel better about themselves.

Do teens want to succeed for the prize or for the pride?

Communities will benefit, too. Better-educated students make better citizens. One Florida educator explains why she is **supportive** of rewards as motivation. "We're not buying grades," she says. "The students must do the work. We're rewarding the progress students make in taking responsibility and working toward goals. And we're helping to boost their self-esteem."

Kids tend to agree. "I feel good that I can make those kinds of grades," a high-school student said. She admits that she first got involved in her school's rewards program for prizes like TVs and cars. Now, though, she enjoys trying hard.

In the Chicago area, leaders wanted to raise the rates of high-school graduation for Latino students. The leaders wanted more Latino kids to go to college. They began offering $500 college scholarships to high-school freshmen who promised to graduate. A student named Gilberto got one of the scholarships. "I think it was the most important factor in my applying to college," he says. "It really motivated me to do [well] every single year of high school."

College scholarship money may motivate teens to finish high school.

DRAWBACKS OF REWARDS What issue could there be with communities paying kids to succeed? It seems as if everybody wins. A number of educators and community leaders strongly disagree, however. They raise some cautions.

Rewards do not really change behavior. Studies show that students may perform well for rewards for a while. They will go back to doing poorly, however, if they do not win every time.

Rewards lose their appeal. If you are rewarded every time you do something, being rewarded may get boring. You might stop

participating. The reward may lose its power to motivate.

Rewards discourage learning. Students who succeed for external, or outer, rewards, like money or prizes, do not really learn much. They do not enjoy learning for its own sake.

Rewards are too competitive. Some students cannot improve their grades or test scores, no matter how many TVs or cars you dangle in front of them. They are already doing their best, even if it is not the best in their class. It is unfair to set them up as losers.

PRIDE AS MOTIVATION Rewards like money and prizes are *extrinsic.* That is, they come from outside you. Many experts **believe,** however, that the best motivation is *intrinsic*—coming from within. People who have intrinsic motivation see a real **connection** between their own efforts and their success. They take responsibility for what they do, whether or not the community rewards them. The resulting pride, some people say, lasts longer than anything money can buy.

WRAP IT UP

Find It on the Page

1. How do communities benefit from student success?

2. What two aims did Chicago-area leaders want to accomplish by giving Latino students scholarship money?

3. List two possible drawbacks of using rewards as motivation.

Use Clues

4. Are there ways communities can lose by giving rewards to students? Explain.

5. What evidence does the article offer to support the argument that rewards are a good idea?

6. How can communities support students with both extrinsic and intrinsic motivation?

Connect to the Big Question

After reading this article, what would you say to someone who believed that your community should pay kids to succeed?

Real-Life Connection

Do you use slang? What do you think about it? Copy the word web below on your own paper. Use it to jot down your ideas about slang.

Slang

community (kuh MYOO nuh tee) *noun*   A **community** is a group of people who live in the same place or share the same interests.
EXAMPLE: *Dr. Chavez is well-respected in the medical **community**.*

culture (KUHL chuhr) *noun*   **Culture** is the way of life that people in a particular group share.
EXAMPLE: *Fourth of July fireworks are a tradition in U.S. **culture**.*

figure (FI gyuhr) *verb*   When you **figure** something out, you come to understand it.
EXAMPLE: *I hope my brother does not **figure** out what I am getting him for his birthday.*

group (groop) *noun*   A **group** is a collection of people or things treated as a single item.
EXAMPLE: *Shara thinks chocolate should be its own food **group**.*

isolate (Y suh layt) *verb*   To **isolate** is to separate out or to leave alone.
EXAMPLE: *Do not **isolate** the new kid at the lunch table.*

THE BIG ?

How much do our communities shape us?

You wake up one morning, and everyone is speaking a nonsense language. How do you feel? How much of your sense of belonging to a community comes from understanding others, and being understood by them? As you read the article, ask yourself: **How do our communities shape the way we speak and write?**

How Teens Use Slang

You say the band is *sick*. Your dad might have said his favorite band was *awesome*. Your grandfather might have said *groovy*. You might not be able to **figure** out one another's slang terms. All three of you, though, would be saying you liked a band. Most slang terms come and go quickly. Some stay around. All three generations, for example, would probably agree that music is *cool*.

Slang is informal language shared by a **group.** It is not just different generations that use different slang terms. Various professions have their own slang. You can hear it if you watch TV medical or police shows. A **culture** can also have its own slang. **Cultural** slang often mixes English terms with those from another language. When many people think about slang, however, they think about teenagers. Young people in various eras have had their own slang.

REASONS FOR SLANG Slang serves a number of purposes. Slang can make it easier for members of a work **community** to do their jobs. A surgeon in an operating room can say, "Scalpel, stat!" The assisting nurse understands what the surgeon means: "Hand me that sharp, sterilized knife. Now!"

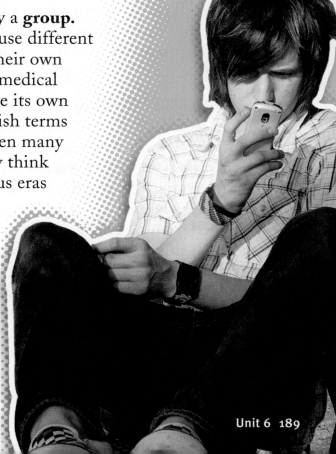

When teens send text messages, they often use slang.

In the age of Internet communications, slang can be a shortcut language. E-mail, instant messaging, and text messaging have their own form of code. Letters and numbers stand for whole words. You want to communicate quickly and save on cell phone charges. *What's up?* becomes *Sup?* You type *CUL8R* instead of writing out *I will see you later.*

According to experts, however, the most important reason people use slang is to show who they are. People who share a **communal** language feel as if they are insiders. This is especially true for teens. Language researcher Tony Thorne explains it this way: "Language is very important to teenagers, because it's another badge of identity." The flip side of using slang to fit in is using it to **isolate** others. People who do not understand your slang are left out. Thorne says using slang this way makes teens feel powerful: "Teens can use words that older people and outsiders can't understand. There is this sense that they're really in control."

> People who share a communal language feel as if they are insiders.

WORRIES ABOUT SLANG Some parents and teachers are concerned about teen slang. Parents may wonder if kids are using code terms to hide drug use or other risky behaviors. Teachers sometimes ban slang from classrooms. These teachers think using slang keeps students from learning how to write and speak well in Standard English.

Some kids may use slang or code to keep their activities **isolated** from parents' awareness. Many young people, however, say they are not using slang or Internet code to hide criminal activity. They just want to have a language of their own.

Teachers may be worrying without reason, too. Researchers in England studied kids who use lots of Internet slang. The students actually did just fine on tests of traditional spelling and grammar. Many teens who use slang also know how to do what language researchers call "code-switching." When you code-switch, you use slang with your friends. You switch to Standard English in school and other formal situations.

BREAKING THE CODE Parents and other adults sometimes try to break the code of teen slang. They might check online slang dictionaries, **figuring** they will get a translation. Many teens find these dictionaries laughable, however. When a Boston newspaper ran a "guide" to teen slang, the column got more than eighty comments from kids. The teens had never heard of many of the terms. Other terms were hopelessly outdated. Teen slang changes too quickly for adults to keep up.

Kids find it just plain embarrassing when adults try to use teen slang themselves. One recent TV ad pokes fun at parents who break into teen slang. "I'm cool with that," a mother tells her teen son. He rolls his eyes. "I don't think you're cool enough to say *cool with that*," he answers.

WRAP IT UP

Find It on the Page

1. According to experts, what is the most important reason people use slang?

2. What is "code-switching"?

3. What is one reason parents are concerned about teen slang?

Use Clues

4. Are there times when teens use slang to isolate not just parents, but other teens? Explain.

5. Should kids be allowed to use common slang terms or codes in writing for school? Why or why not?

6. Why is "code-switching" an important skill? How might it affect a person's success?

Connect to the Big Question

After reading this article, how big a part would you say communities play in shaping an individual's language?

Real-Life Connection

Take a moment to think of your favorite ads. Are they on TV, the radio, the Internet, or in print? What do you like about them? Most importantly, do they actually affect what you purchase? Jot down your thoughts in response to these questions.

Check It Out

Marketing is the process of convincing people to buy products.

- TV commercials, magazine ads, and music videos are all tools used by marketers.
- In 2007, for example, advertisers spent $1.2 billion for ads on social networking sites, such as MySpace, that are popular with teens.

WORD BANK

always (AWL wayz) *adverb*   If you **always** do something, you do it every time.
EXAMPLE: *Shonda **always** orders thin-crust pizza.*

connection (kuh NEK shuhn) *noun*   A **connection** is a link between two things, people, or ideas.
EXAMPLE: *The coach explained the **connection** between exercise and fitness.*

family (FAM lee) *noun*   A **family** is a group whose members have something in common or are related.
EXAMPLE: *Ray's **family** gets together for a big reunion picnic every summer.*

influence (IN floo uhns) *noun*   An **influence** is the effect that someone or something has on you.
EXAMPLE: *Zoe started taking flute lessons because of her aunt's **influence**.*

values (VAL yooz) *noun*   Your **values** are the ideas you believe are important.
EXAMPLE: *Cheating goes against my **values**.*

How much do our communities shape us?

Your friend just got a new MP3 player with money he earned. When he brings it to a party, some other kids say it is not the right brand. Now your friend feels stupid. What would you say to him? As you read the article, ask yourself: How does advertising affect teens?

Buying Power

You might not realize it, but advertisers are listening to you. People who sell products want to know what matters to you—what you cannot live without. If you do not have an opinion right now, do not worry. Advertisers will try to help you make up your mind.

Why does the marketing industry care so much about you? Whether you recognize it or not, you are incredibly powerful. Teens in the United States have a combined buying power of almost $300 billion a year. You might look into your wallet and say, "No way." Do not underestimate your **influence,** though. The money kids spend, and the **family** purchases they affect, help drive the American economy.

BRAND LOYALTY Advertisers target teens for one reason. You are open to developing what is called "brand loyalty." If you decide that a product is great, you are likely to continue buying it and tell others about it. You will buy new products from the same company.

▲
Attention teens: Advertisers want you!

You can probably name your favorite brands of soft drinks and music players right off the top of your head. You and your **family** may not be able to afford your top brand choices, but these products still rank first on your list. Advertisers want their brands on that list.

Your brand choices in many areas are so **influential** that people of all ages follow them. Kids like you decide what is in. Advertisers are watching your age group's every move. They spend money to find out how to make you spend yours.

IT'S A VIRUS Marketers are moving beyond traditional advertising. They know you watch TV commercials and see magazine ads. They know you are suspicious of these old ways of pushing products. Today's marketers reach out to find you.

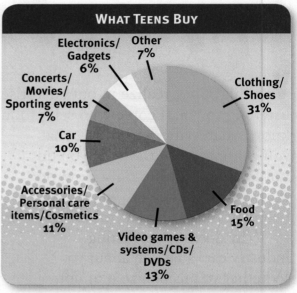

WHAT TEENS BUY

- Electronics/Gadgets 6%
- Other 7%
- Concerts/Movies/Sporting events 7%
- Car 10%
- Accessories/Personal care items/Cosmetics 11%
- Clothing/Shoes 31%
- Food 15%
- Video games & systems/CDs/DVDs 13%

Information is from Piper Jaffray, "Taking Stock with Teens Survey," Fall 2007.

They are putting products and brand names right into movies, TV shows, and video games. They hit you with pop-ups on the Internet. They send text messages or sign onto MySpace as a pretend friend. They make funny videos and post them on Web sites. The videos are ads in disguise. You laugh at a clip, download it, and send it to six of your friends. The message spreads like a cold virus. This new kind of advertising is called "viral marketing." It makes use of the **connection** between kids everywhere.

WHY IT WORKS "Wait!" you might say. "I am too smart to fall for that phony stuff!" Advertisers know better. One professor who studies the media says, "Advertising has **always** sold anxiety, and it certainly sells anxiety to the young. It's **always** telling them they're losers unless they're cool."

Wearing, eating, and listening to **familiar** brands might be more important to you than you want to admit. It is comforting to know that you fit with the people around you. The things you own can help accomplish that. It takes a lot to go against the flow. Some people do it because they have to: they cannot afford popular products. Others do it because they want to. You may believe it is wrong to judge people by how much money they have, or how they look, or what they own. Acting on those **values,** however, can be hard. That is exactly what marketers count on.

FIGHTING BACK Can you beat the advertisers at their own game? Some people suggest becoming an educated consumer, or purchaser of products. Look at the messages behind the ads. What are you really being sold? Learn to **disconnect** the product from the image that marketers want you to buy. Try making choices based on what is most **valuable** to you. Be on guard against viral marketing. Use all that buying power wisely. Advertisers will be listening. Every once in a while, they may hear you say, "No, thanks!"

WRAP IT UP

Find It on the Page

1. How much combined buying power do U.S. teens have?

2. How did viral marketing get its name?

3. According to the pie chart, in what product area do teens spend most of their money?

Use Clues

4. What makes young teens so open to advertising messages?

5. Should teens be able to spend their money any way they want? Explain.

6. How could your school or community help kids become educated consumers?

Connect to the Big Question

After reading this article, how much influence do you think advertisers have on who you are? Explain your answer.

Real-Life Connection

What do you think of when you hear the word *age*? How about the word *beauty*? Copy the word webs below and jot down your thoughts.

Age   **Beauty**

WORD BANK

claim (klaym) *verb*   When you **claim** something, you state that you believe it is true.
EXAMPLE: *Do you really **claim** that your team can beat ours?*

common (KAH muhn) *adjective*   Something that is **common** is ordinary or shared by a number of people.
EXAMPLE: *Vanilla is a **common** ice cream choice.*

culture (KUHL chuhr) *noun*   **Culture** is the way of life that people in a particular group share.
EXAMPLE: *Holiday celebrations often depend on a **culture**.*

generation (je nuh RAY shuhn) *noun*   A **generation** is a group of people who are about the same age.
EXAMPLE: *Today's teens are sometimes called the millennial **generation**.*

history (HIS tuh ree) *noun*   **History** is an account of things that happened in the past.
EXAMPLE: *This summer was the warmest in the **history** of our region.*

How much do our communities shape us?

Someone calls your grandmother beautiful. You are surprised. Her hair is graying and she wears plus-size clothes. Maybe that person needs to rethink the definition of *beautiful*—or maybe you do. As you read the article, ask yourself: Where do we get our ideas about age and beauty?

AGE AND BEAUTY

What two words describe someone who is beautiful? In today's American **culture,** the answer would have to be *young* and *thin*. Watch TV or page through a magazine. You will get the same message over and over again. Ads emphasize the importance of youth and slimness, often beyond belief. Women in their twenties are shown worrying about wrinkles. Young teen fashion models strut down the runways on legs as skinny as twigs.

Ads like these are designed to sell products. However, they also sell a message. The ads **claim** that it is great to be young and thin. Unfortunately, they also say it is awful to be anything other than young and thin.

Think about the effects of messages like these. Most people do not look like models. Comparing yourself with people in ads can make you feel bad about your body image. It is **common,** for example, to find girls even as young as five or six worrying about getting "too fat." Kids in kindergarten already have negative stereotypes of older people.

▲ Does beauty have an age limit?

DIFFERENT MODELS Where do ideas about beauty come from in the first place? You might be surprised to learn that people in different times and places have defined *beauty* differently. For example, plump people have more **commonly** been considered beautiful than skinny people. Just look at the paintings and statues in an art museum! For most of human **history,** people had to struggle to feed themselves. Those who carried a little more weight were seen as healthier, more successful, and more attractive.

Attitudes about aging can differ **culturally,** too. In many parts of the world, older people are seen as wise and productive members of the community. People do not fear growing older. They welcome it. Younger people value what older people have to offer. In Korea, for example, people celebrate Respect for the Elders Week every year.

> False media images of beauty can lead to harmful stereotypes.

FEAR OF AGING, FEAR OF YOUTH False media images of beauty can lead to harmful stereotypes. This is true on both sides of the **generation** gap. When you think of being elderly, what images come to mind? Many kids associate old age with weakness, disability, and fading mental abilities.

"Negative stereotypes of aging are found in many aspects of our **culture,** from casual conversations to television advertisements," says Dr. Becca Levy, who studies aging. "Ads often present the elderly as either close to childhood or close to death." If you think of aging as a negative thing, you probably will not want to spend time with older people. If you do not spend time with them, you will not get to know them as real individuals. You might even be afraid of them.

The reverse is also true. Studies show that many older people are uncomfortable around teens. Older people may have their own negative stereotypes about you. To some older people, you seem loud, rude, irresponsible, spoiled, and ignorant. They might not want to spend time with you, either.

DANCING THE STEREOTYPES AWAY Do you have to accept the media's messages about age and beauty? Not necessarily, say some people. Some communities are finding ways to change attitudes by bringing teens and senior citizens together. **Intergenerational** activities are making a difference.

For example, in some communities, high schools throw "Senior Citizen Proms." Teens and elderly people dress up and share refreshments. They even learn each other's dances. "I think the proms have broken down some stereotypes on both sides," one organizer says. "Everyone seems to have a lot of fun. I know the seniors enjoy talking with the young people." Brooke Taylor, a teen who attended a Senior Citizen Prom, agrees. "I realize that senior citizens can have fun, too. And they really know how to party! Not all older people just sit in wheelchairs and rockers all the time." Events that allow **generations** to mix also allow them to understand each other. Now *that* is beautiful.

WRAP IT UP

Find It on the Page

1. According to the article, what two words do most Americans use to define *beauty*?

2. Why has plumpness historically been considered more beautiful than thinness?

3. Describe two stereotypes older people have about teens.

Use Clues

4. Give one example of how media images of beauty might have a harmful effect.

5. What is one way your community could help teens and older people get over their negative stereotypes about one another?

6. In your opinion, do teens and older people have important things to learn from one another? Explain.

Connect to the Big Question

After reading this article, have your ideas about age and beauty changed? Explain.

UNIT 6 WRAP UP

PROJECT: **Write-Around**

 Answer the Big Question: How much do our communities shape us?

You have read about people in their communities. Now, use what you learned to answer the Unit 6 Big Question (BQ).

STEP 1: Form a Group and Choose

Your first step is to pick Unit 6 articles that you like.

Get together. Find a small group to work with.

Read the list of articles. Discuss which articles listed on the left side of this page were the most interesting to you.

Choose two or more articles. Pick articles that you all agree on.

STEP 2: Reread and Answer the Unit Big Question

Your next step is to answer the Unit BQ in your group.

Reread the articles you chose. As you reread, think about what the Unit BQ means.

Answer questions. Before you reread each article, discuss these questions with your group:

- What does the article tell us about communities?
- According to the article, how might our communities shape what we do? How might they shape how we think?
- How does this article help readers understand the influence that a community can have on its members?

Take notes. Write the Unit BQ at the top of a blank sheet of paper to begin a write-around. Pass the paper around the group. Each member has 1 minute to write his or her answer. Leave space after each response to add notes from step 3.

STEP 3: Discuss and Give Reasons

In this step, talk about your Unit BQ answer in your group.

Discuss your answers to the Unit BQ. Explain your answer to the group. Use details from the articles to explain your answer. Add to your notes as each group member speaks.

STEP 4: Summarize the Group's Response

Now, finish the write-around by creating a summary.

Reread your group's answers. Look over your notes and see if group members generally agreed on the answer. If they do not agree, the summary should give reasons for all views.

Summarize the write-around. Be sure that viewpoints are supported with reasons. Write the most important ideas from the write-around, not all of the ideas.

STEP 5: Check and Fix

Next, you and your group will look over your write-around summary to see if it could be improved.

Use the rubric. Use the questions to evaluate your work. Answer each question yes or no. You might trade summaries with another group to check its work and get another opinion about yours.

Discuss your evaluations. For your yes answers, think about what you can do to make your summary even stronger. If you have any no answers, talk about what you can do to turn each no into a yes.

Improve your summary. After discussing your summary by using the rubric, work together to make your summary stronger.

STEP 6: Practice and Present

Get ready to present your write-around and summary.

Practice what you want to say. You will use your write-around to explain your group's answer to the Unit BQ. Each group member might present his or her answer, and then one member might present the summary.

Present your work. Explain your answer to the Unit 6 BQ to your classmates. You might discuss it with them, or you might post your thoughts about the Unit BQ on a classroom Web page or in a blog.

RUBRIC

Does the summary . . .
- answer the Unit BQ?
- include details from at least two articles in Unit 6?
- show a clear relationship between the answer and the reasons given to support it?
- include the viewpoints of all group members, even if group members disagreed?
- show clear organization of the answer and supporting details?

GLOSSARY

This glossary will help you quickly find definitions of Word Bank words.

A

always (AWL wayz) *adverb*   If you always do something, you do it every time.

appearance (uh PIR uhns) *noun* **Appearance** is the way someone or something looks or seems to be.

argue (AHR gyoo) *verb*   To **argue** with someone is to disagree with the person in a discussion.

argument (AHR gyuh muhnt) *noun*   An **argument** is a reason or set of reasons you give for being in favor of or against something.

arrange (uh RAYNJ) *verb*   To **arrange** objects means to put them in a suitable order.

audience (AW dee uhns) *noun*   An **audience** is a group that listens to or watches a performance.

B

battle (BA tuhl) *noun*   A **battle** is a fight or struggle.

belief (buh LEEF) *noun*   A **belief** is an idea that one feels is true or important.

body (BAH dee) *noun*   The **body** is the physical form or main portion of something.

C

calculate (KAL kyuh layt) *verb*   When you **calculate,** you use math to find an answer, or you plan carefully.

challenge (CHA luhnj) *noun*   A **challenge** is a difficult situation to deal with.

claim (klaym) *verb*   When you **claim** something, you state that you believe it is true.

class (klas) *noun*   A **class** is a group of students who meet with a teacher regularly to study the same subject.

clue (kloo) *noun*   A **clue** is a piece of information that helps you find an answer.

common (KAH muhn) *adjective* Something that is **common** is ordinary or shared by a number of people.

communicate (kuh MYOO nuh kayt) *verb*   When you **communicate,** you pass on information so that it is understood.

community (kuh MYOO nuh tee) *noun* A **community** is a group of people who live in the same place or share the same interests.

compete (kuhm PEET) *verb* When you **compete,** you try to win against someone else.

concept (KAHN sept) *noun* A **concept** is a general idea you have about something, based on information.

conclude (kuhn KLOOD) *verb* You **conclude** something when you make a decision using the available information.

confirm (kuhn FUHRM) *verb* To **confirm** something means to make sure it is true.

connection (kuh NEK shuhn) *noun* A **connection** is a link between two things, people, or ideas.

conscious (KAHN shuhs) *adjective* When you make a **conscious** effort, you do something on purpose.

consequence (KAHN suh kwens) *noun* A **consequence** is the outcome of a choice.

constant (KAHN stuhnt) *adjective* Something that happens over and over on a regular basis is **constant**.

convince (kuhn VINS) *verb* You **convince** people of something when you get them to agree with you.

correspond (kawr uh SPAHND) *verb* When two things **correspond,** they match, are in harmony, or are alike in meaning or purpose.

culture (KUHL chuhr) *noun* **Culture** is the way of life that people in a particular group share.

custom (KUHS tuhm) *noun* A **custom** is the usual way to do something.

D

decision (di SI zhuhn) *noun* When you make a choice about something, you make a **decision**.

defend (di FEND) *verb* To **defend** is to protect someone or something from danger.

demand (di MAND) *verb* When you **demand** something, you ask for it as a right.

depend (di PEND) *verb* When you **depend** on someone, you count on that person for support.

determine (di TUHR muhn) *verb* When you reach a decision about something, you **determine** what to do.

devise (di VYZ) *verb* To **devise** means to plan, invent, or create.

dialogue (DY uh lawg) *noun*
Dialogue is conversation between two or more people.

direction (duh REK shuhn) *noun*
To go in a **direction** is to follow a certain path.

discover (dis KUH vuhr) *verb* To **discover** something is to see it or understand it for the first time.

distinguish (di STING wish) *verb* To **distinguish** between two things means to tell the difference between them.

diverse (dy VUHRS) *adjective* Things that are **diverse** are different from one another, or show variety.

E

establish (i STA blish) *verb* You **establish** something when you put it in place or create it.

evidence (E vuh duhns) *noun*
Evidence is any sign that something exists.

examine (ig ZA muhn) *verb* To **examine** something is to look closely at it to learn facts.

expectations (ek spek TAY shuhnz) *noun* **Expectations** are hopes for the future.

explain (ik SPLAYN) *verb* You **explain** something when you give its reason or background.

expression (ik SPRE shuhn) *noun* An **expression** is an outward showing of a feeling or thought.

F

fact (fakt) *noun* A **fact** is something that is true.

family (FAM lee) *noun* A **family** is a group whose members have something in common or are related.

fantasy (FAN tuh see) *noun* Something you imagine is a **fantasy**.

fiction (FIK shuhn) *noun* Something that is **fiction** is not true.

figure (FI gyuhr) *verb* When you **figure** something out, you come to understand it.

form (fawrm) *verb* You **form** something when you organize it or make it come together.

form (fawrm) *noun* The **form** of something is its design or shape.

G

game (gaym) *noun* A **game** is an activity with a winner that people do for fun or sport.

generation (je nuh RAY shuhn) *noun* A **generation** is a group of people who are about the same age.

gesture (JES chuhr) *noun*   A **gesture** is an action or a movement of the body that expresses an idea or a feeling.

group (groop) *noun*   A **group** is a collection of people or things treated as a single item.

guess (ges) *verb*   When you **guess** something, you form an opinion of it without having all the information about it.

H

history (HIS tuh ree) *noun*   **History** is an account of things that happened in the past.

I

ideals (y DEELZ) *noun*   **Ideals** are beliefs or standards of behavior that people use to measure their actions.

imitate (I muh tayt) *verb*   You act the same as other people when you **imitate** them.

individuality (in duh vi juh WA luh tee) *noun*   Your **individuality** is the mix of qualities that makes you different from other people.

influence (IN floo uhns) *noun*   An **influence** is the effect that someone or something has on you.

instructions (in STRUHK shuhnz) *noun*   **Instructions** are directions telling you what to do.

integrate (IN tuh grayt) *verb*   To **integrate** means to bring different parts together to make a whole.

intently (in TENT lee) *adverb*   To do something **intently** is to do it with strong focus.

investigate (in VES tuh gayt) *verb*   To **investigate** something is to look at it carefully to find solutions or answers.

involve (in VAHLV) *verb*   To **involve** is to include or to have as a part of something.

isolate (Y suh layt) *verb*   To **isolate** is to separate out or to leave alone.

issue (I shoo) *noun*   An **issue** is an important problem people are working to solve.

J

judge (juhj) *verb*   When you **judge**, you form an opinion or make a decision based on facts.

K

knowledge (NAH lij) *noun*   **Knowledge** is information that has been learned.

L

language (LANG gwij) *noun*   **Language** is a system used to communicate, such as a set of words or signs.

limit (LI muht) *noun*   A **limit** is a point beyond which something does not exist or is no longer possible.

logical (LAH ji kuhl) *adjective*   Something is **logical** when it makes sense, follows the rules, or is expected.

lose (looz) *verb*   When you **lose**, you fail to reach your goal.

M

measure (ME zhuhr) *verb*   When you **measure** something, you find out its extent or size.

message (ME sij) *noun*   A **message** is information that you give someone in writing or by a signal.

method (ME thuhd) *noun*   A **method** is a way of doing something.

N

narrow (NER oh) *adjective*   If you are **narrow** in thinking or choosing, you have a hard time being open to new ideas.

negotiate (ni GOH shee ayt) *verb*   You **negotiate** when you talk with someone else to solve a problem through give and take.

nonverbal (nahn VUHR buhl) *adjective*   Something that is **nonverbal** uses no words.

notice (NOH tuhs) *verb*   To **notice** something is to become aware of it.

O

observe (uhb ZUHRV) *verb*   When you **observe** someone or something, you watch the person or thing carefully.

opinion (uh PIN yuhn) *noun*   An **opinion** is a belief based on facts and experience.

order (AWR duhr) *noun*   The **order** of something is how it is arranged.

organize (AWR guh nyz) *verb*   When you **organize**, you put separate parts into some kind of order.

P

participation (pahr ti suh PAY shuhn) *noun*   **Participation** is taking part in something with others.

pattern (PA tuhrn) *noun*   A **pattern** is a repeated series of events or details that you can identify.

perform (puhr FAWRM) *verb*   To **perform** is to do something that requires special skills, in front of an audience.

personality (puhr suh NA luh tee) *noun*   Someone's **personality** is the collection of emotions and behaviors that makes the person who he or she is.

perspective (puhr SPEK tiv) *noun*   Your **perspective** is your point of view, or the way you see and understand something.

prepare (pri PER) *verb*   To **prepare** is to plan or get ready for something.

presume (pri ZOOM) *verb*   To **presume** is to expect that something will be a certain way without proof.

probably (PRAH buh blee) *adverb*   To say something will **probably** happen means you are pretty sure it will happen.

prove (proov) *verb*   When you show that something is true, you **prove** it.

purpose (PUHR puhs) *noun*   A **purpose** is the reason that something exists or is done.

Q

question (KWES chuhn) *noun*   A **question** is something that is asked.

quote (kwoht) *verb*   To **quote** someone is to repeat his or her exact words.

R

reaction (ree AK shuhn) *noun*   A **reaction** is something that happens in answer to something else.

realistic (ree uh LIS tik) *adjective*   Something that is true to life is **realistic**.

refer (ri FUHR) *verb*   To **refer** to something is to direct attention to it.

reflect (ri FLEKT) *verb*   When you **reflect** on something, you give it serious thought.

report (ri PAWRT) *noun*   A **report** is a statement of facts.

resist (ri ZIST) *verb*   To **resist** something is to struggle against it.

resolve (ri ZAHLV) *verb*   To **resolve** something is to find an answer or solution to it.

respond (ri SPAHND) *verb*   When you **respond**, you answer a question or do something in return.

reveal (ri VEEL) *verb*   To **reveal** means to make something known that was hidden.

S

search (suhrch) *verb*   When you **search** for something, you look carefully to try to find it.

share (sher) *verb*   When people **share** something, each person gets a part of it.

similar (SI muh luhr) *adjective*   Things that are **similar** are alike in some way.

source (sawrs) *noun* A **source** is a person, place, or thing that supplies something.

study (STUH dee) *verb* You **study** a subject when you read about it and think about it.

study (STUH dee) *noun* Scientists conduct a **study** when they test an idea or research a subject.

support (suh PAWRT) *verb* To **support** something is to show that it is true, to be in favor of it, or to help it succeed.

survey (SUHR vay) *noun* A **survey** is a way to gather information about a topic by asking questions.

survival (suhr VY vuhl) *noun* **Survival** means to stay alive in difficult situations.

symbolize (SIM buh lyz) *verb* To **symbolize** means to use one thing to represent another thing, usually an idea.

T

test (test) *verb* You **test** something when you try it to find out information.

trend (trend) *noun* A **trend** is a pattern of activity or a popular style.

true (troo) *adjective* Something that is real, and not false, is **true**.

U

unbelievable (uhn buh LEE vuh buhl) *adjective* Something that is **unbelievable** seems unlikely to be true.

unique (yoo NEEK) *adjective* Something is described as **unique** when it is one of a kind or very unusual.

V

values (VAL yooz) *noun* Your **values** are the ideas you believe are important.

verbal (VUHR buhl) *adjective* Something that is **verbal** uses words.

visual (VI zhuh wuhl) *adjective* Something **visual** can be seen or understood through sight.

win (win) *verb* When you **win** something, you beat another person or team in a contest or you reach your goal.

INDEX

Use the index to find out more about real life topics.

CREDITS

Illustrations

Miracle Studios 2-3, 38-39, 74-75, 110-111, 146-147, 166-167.

Photographs

Every effort has been made to secure permission and provide appropriate credit for photographic material. The publisher deeply regrets any omission and pledges to correct errors called to its attention in subsequent editions.

Unless otherwise acknowledged, all photographs are the property of Pearson Education, Inc.

Photo locators denoted as follows: Top (T), Center (C), Bottom (B), Left (L), Right (R), Background (Bkgd)

Cover (Bkgd L) Glowimages/Getty Images, (Bkgd R) Purestock/Alamy, (L) Fancy Photography/Veer, (CL) Jon Feingersh/Blend Images/Getty Images, (CR) Bec Parsons/Getty Images, (R) Compassionate Eye Foundation/Drew Kelly/Digital Vision/Getty Images; 5 Dan Brandenburg/iStockphoto; 9 Chris Schmidt/iStockphoto; 10 Juan Estey/iStockphoto; 13 Randolph Pamphrey/iStockphoto; 17 Robert E Daemmrich/Getty Images; 21 Bartlomiej Stroinski/Big Stock Photo; 25 Corbis Premium RF/Alamy; 26 Chris Schmidt/iStockphoto; 29 Miodrag Gajic/iStockphoto; 30 Marc Brown/iStockphoto; 33 Cathy Keifer/iStockphoto; 34 Davis Lewis/iStockphoto; 41 Phil Cole/Getty Images; 45 Jim Pruitt/iStockphoto; 49 John Zich/Getty Images; 50 Jim Lopes/Shutterstock; 53 Mark Rose/iStockphoto; 57 Mike Liu/Shutterstock; 58 Michael Loccisano/Getty Images; 61 Koson Kajeekailas/iStockphoto; 62 WizData, Inc/Shutterstock; 65 Bettina Baumgartner/Shutterstock; 66 Jim Cummins/Taxi/Gety Images; 69 Maciej Laska/iStockphoto; 77 Simon McConico/iStockphoto; 81 Robert Deal/iStockphotol; 82 Forest Woodward/iStockphoto; 85 Library of Congress; 89 iStockphoto; 93 Mark Coffey/iStockphoto; 94 Cyril Laubscher/Arena-PAL Images; 97 Bettmann/Corbis; 98 David Maxwell/Stringer/Getty Images; 101 Irina Smirnova/iStockphoto; 102 Ferran Traite Soler/iStockphoto; 105 Timothy A. Clary/Getty Images; 113 Kati Neudert/iStockphoto; 117 Danger Jacobs/Shutterstock; 118 AP Images; 121 Miodrag Gaijic/iStockphoto; 125 Cat London/iStockphoto; 129 Christian Carroll/iStockphoto; 133 Ryan KC Wong/iStockphoto; 134 Izabela Habur/iStockphoto; 137 Christle's Images/Corbis; 138 Shutterstock; 141 The Kobal Collection; 149 Marcus Brandt/Getty Images; 150 Supri Suharjoto/Shutterstock; 153 Brian & Vildan Chase/Shutterstock; 157 TAOLMOR/Shutterstock; 158 Clay Blackburn/iStockphoto; 161 Bettmann/Corbis; 162 Linda Kloosterhof/iStockphoto; 169 Benny Gool/AP Images; 170 Eraxion/Big Stock Photo; 171 Shutterstock; 177 Chris Schmidt/iStockphoto; 181 (T) Alan Freed/Shutterstock, (B) Eric Gevaert/Shutterstock; 182 M. Dillon/Corbis; 185 iStockphoto; 186 Stephen Coburn/Shutterstock; 189 James Pauls/iStockphoto; 193 Supri Suharjoto/Shutterstock; 197 iStockphoto.